MW00510355

THE TAX DETECTIVE

UNCOVERING
THE MYSTERY OF
SMALL BUSINESS
TAX PLANNING

Featuring America's Top Certified Tax Coaches
Foreword by **DOMINIQUE MOLINA, CPA CTC**

Published by Certified Tax Coach,™ LLC, Las Vegas, NV

Certified Tax Coach™ is a registered trademark

Printed in the United States of America.

ISBN: 978-0-9832341-5-9

For more information, please write:

Certified Tax Coach, LLC™,
8885 Rio San Diego Drive Ste 237
San Diego, CA 92108

or call 1.888.582.9752

Visit us online at www.CertifiedTaxCoach.com

TABLE OF CONTENTS

What Is a Tax Detective?

By Dominique Molina, CPA CTC

There are two basic concepts in aspiring to make more money. First, you can seek to earn more. Yet this presents a challenge as most people *are* seeking to earn more, yet most rarely do so. Seeking to earn more is an arduous and unpredictable process. What will you do? How will you do it? When will you do it? You can *say* you'd like to earn more money, but the question is, "*can* you earn more money?" On the other hand, you can choose a defensive approach. Financial *defense* is spending less. For most Americans, taxes are our biggest expense. Therefore, it makes sense to focus your financial defense where you spend the most. Financial defense, particularly in the area of tax planning guarantees results. You can spend all sorts of time, effort, and money promoting your business or working towards promotions at work. But that can't guarantee results.

So how do you reduce your tax and keep more of what you earn? Or even better, how can you earn more without paying tax? These questions can be answered by looking to the wisest investors and financial experts for advice.

The tax code is close to 74,000 pages long and contains a mind boggling 5 million words. (To give you a comparison, War and Peace is only 1,444 pages and the Bible has just over 788,000 words.) Looking for rules and benefits in the tax code can be like a mystery book... a particularly *long* mystery book.

But if you want to keep more of what you earn, it's important to identify the clues to a lower tax bill. In this mission, professional tax planners act much like detectives identifying the benefits and piecing together the strategy that will bring you the biggest amount of savings.

Like any mystery, taxes can be solved with a bit of detective work, and there is no better detective for the case than a Certified Tax Coach. By serving as your financial advisor, a Certified Tax Coach can sleuth out the best opportunities for keeping more of your money in your pocket and growing the value of your investments.

Of course, there is no such thing as a real "tax detective," but a smart tax advisor shares many qualities with the best detectives:

- A willingness to look beyond the obvious.
- A hunger for answers.
- A desire to help people.
- An encyclopedic knowledge of the law.
- ProActive problem-solving skills.

By being creative and looking beyond the standard or accepted way of doing things, a tax detective can uncover many opportunities that other tax professionals miss. This translates to better results for you as you'll be able to trim expenses and put more of your pre-tax dollars to work on the things that are important to you, like your home, your family, your hobbies.

The authors of this book are some of the top Certified Tax Coaches across the country; detectives in the mystery of paying less tax. They are tax professionals who scour the tax code and thoroughly examine their client's income and business options to rescue every deduction, tax advantage, and credit possible. Certified Tax Coaches emphasize year-round proactive planning to ensure that business owners can utilize every available loophole and savings opportunity possible; and they've come together to share these ideas with you.

You may find it helpful to skip chapters and focus on the topics most meaningful to your business. If you're feeling up to the task, you can even become a bit of a tax detective yourself and follow the clues outlined for you by the authors of this book. You just may surprise yourself when pieces come together to stimulate your thinking about how you might apply what you learn to your own situation!

In any case, I hope each time you re-read, *The Tax Detective*, you'll find something new and useful to help you work proactively to minimize your greatest expense and grow your wealth. After all, you may have 99 problems, but the IRS doesn't have to be one. You can manage your business well and learn powerful, legal tax strategies to pay your taxes honestly, while keeping money in your pocket.

Let the investigation begin,

Dominique Molina

Tax Breaks Super Sleuth

CHAPTER 1

Benefits of Tax Planning ...Today and Tomorrow

R. Travis Evans, MLERE, ASBC CFP®, CAPP™, CFS®, CLA™, CWPP™, RFC®, CTC

Have you ever had the thrill of finding money hidden somewhere that you'd completely forgotten about? This past November, my wife put on a coat she hadn't worn since the previous winter and found a bank envelope with $120 that she thought she had lost. She was so excited to share that newfound money with another family, blessing them with a wonderful Thanksgiving meal.

What would you do if you found an envelope with your name on it for $15,000? Where would you go? What would you buy? Whom would you invite? Would you spend some and save the rest? Would you share it with family or charity? What if you knew this mysterious envelope would reappear every year with thousands of dollars to be used however you like? Free money. Extra money. Money to put smiles on faces, today—money to help secure college educations, and your own golden years, tomorrow.

Let's be honest with one another: tax planning doesn't sound very exciting, does it? But when you learn about the differences between proactive tax planning and reactive tax preparation, you will soon become excited about the extra, uncovered wealth that otherwise would have been completely wasted and gone, forever. Certified Tax Coaches

1

save their clients an average of $15,000 per year. When you work with your own tax detective to investigate tax-saving opportunities, what will you do with your newfound money?

What Is Tax Planning?

Tax planning goes beyond tax preparation, and it is worth investigating those differences to understand just how valuable a talented tax coach can be. Tax preparation is reactive. It takes information about a company's behaviors throughout the year and uses it to file the tax return, trimming tax costs where possible. A good tax preparer will look for deductions based on a business' activities and take advantage of every possible money-saving strategy, but even the best tax coach can only do so much at the end of the year because a business has already made all of its decisions at that point.

Tax planning is proactive. Instead of waiting passively for a business to make choices and try to find tax solutions that will work with those decisions, tax planners work alongside businesses to make smart choices throughout the year. Instead of trying to make the most of a company's financial choices when it comes time to file, the tax planner will help the business make the most advantageous choices to maximize tax savings at the end of the year.

Tax Strategies Require Advanced Commitment

A proactive tax strategy is about more than income tax. At its best, it is a complete financial plan that can be used for maximizing a company's profits. Every business cares about its bottom line, and taxes make up one of the biggest single expenses of any company. Taxes are also a special consideration because they punish high earnings. You can trim other expenses to keep a low overhead while enjoying high profits, but higher profits will translate to a higher tax burden if you are not careful with your strategy.

Here are a few clues as to why tax strategies need to be made long before it comes time to file taxes:

- A company's business designation greatly affects the way the owner will pay taxes. You might be able to save money by restructuring your business into an S corporation, for example, but you could only benefit from this if your company was restructured early in the tax year.

- You might qualify for deductions on many items that you are unaware of. If you know what deductions you can make, you can let that knowledge guide your spending decisions. Otherwise, you might reach the end of the year, and discover that you spent money on things that couldn't be deducted, while missing valuable deductions elsewhere.

- Moving profits into an investment account can cut down on taxes and save money for the future, but these accounts must be set up correctly and in advance in order to be effective.

- Many other systems and programs can be tax effective, such as setting up an MERP instead of standard group health insurance, but you can't benefit from the tax decrease unless you put the plan to work right away.

At best, a tax preparer who is working reactively might be able to spot these opportunities and advise you about changes for the upcoming year. By that point, though, you have already missed one year of tax benefits. And if tax codes change in the following year, you might be missing out on even more opportunities. You simply cannot save as much money if you are always behind the curve. You need a Certified Tax Coach to guide you through the entire financial year, constantly looking for opportunities, in order to really benefit from a solid tax strategy.

Choosing the Right Tax Planner

The need for a talented tax advisor should be obvious by now. It doesn't take a detective to see that proactive tax planning is more valuable than a passive approach. That is not to say that any financial advisor can fill the role. Just as different doctors have different specialties, and some detectives solve homicides while others investigate jewelry heists, tax professionals differ in their specialties and skills.

Since a tax professional plays such a vital role to the growth of your business, it is worth taking some time to choose the right person for the job. Obviously, finding the right qualifications is the first step. Even an otherwise knowledgeable and well-qualified tax professional can be a bad fit for your needs if he isn't experienced in your industry, or if you don't have a good professional relationship.

If you are looking for a new tax professional, here are a few things to keep in mind:

- Does he or she understand and appreciate the idea of tax planning rather than tax preparation? The ideal financial advisor will have enthusiasm for the idea of proactive tax strategies. If you approach him/her with ideas like those found in this book, he or she should be interested in working with you to find solutions that will fit, rather than dismissing the possibilities without ample consideration.

- Is he or she experienced in your industry? The tax code is complex, and it is impossible to know every possible deduction and loophole for every single industry. It is best to find someone with a proven track record of success with other businesses in your niche. That will ensure that the person helping with your taxes really does know as much as possible about the way tax laws apply to your unique situation.

- Do you have a good personal relationship? Your tax coach will become an integral part of your team. If you don't feel that you can trust your financial planner's advice, you are doing both of you a disservice. Take some time to work with a tax professional before committing to ensure that you get along well and can work together as a good team.

Sometimes, you will find that your current financial advisor is no longer a good fit for your needs. Maybe you have opened a business in a new industry, or your income has grown significantly. It is always possible to "outgrow" your first accountant. When this happens, there is no shame in moving on to another financial planner who will be a better fit. In fact, your current CPA might have a referral ready for a colleague who will be able to take over your account and grow your business to the next level.

One Size Does Not Fit All

Perhaps the most important thing you can do for your business when choosing a financial planner is to pick someone with a great track record in working with companies within your industry or niche. You want someone who has successfully grown businesses that are very similar to yours.

The reason for this is simple: there is no such thing as a one-size-fits-all approach to tax planning, and using strategies that work well for one business might not help your company at all if the industry is different. Different deductions will come up for different businesses and situations, and a person accustomed to working with people from one industry might not think of the opportunities available in another one.

For example, imagine that you are a model. For you, makeup, beauty products, clothing, and hair styling are all business expenses because they are a vital part of being successful at your job. If your accountant comes from a background of working with people who work in home offices, he might not even think about these things when itemizing your deduction. He might be too focused on deductions that may not even be relevant to you simply because those are what he is most accustomed to dealing with.

This does not make him a bad accountant—for an office worker, he might be an ideal tax coach. It is worth taking the time to find a tax planner who knows your industry inside and out and can give you valuable suggestions based on experience.

Tax Planning Is an Ongoing Process

It might be tempting to think of tax planning as something you could do once to "get it out of the way" before turning your focus toward other aspects of your business. After all, once you have made the necessary changes to set your business up for success, you might not feel that having a tax planner on board really makes much difference.

It is true that many parts of a successful tax strategy, like choosing the right business designation, are steps that only need to be implemented once. However, other aspects of your tax strategy will need to be implemented repeatedly, such as identifying and taking advantage of deductions. If you base your entire tax strategy on the deductions taken in a single year, you can potentially miss out on valuable opportunities that crop up later.

More importantly, the tax code is always changing. Just because an opportunity was available a year ago does not necessarily mean it works the same way today. Old loopholes are closed, laws are changed, and new opportunities arise regularly. Strategies that were perfectly viable and legitimate a few years ago might even be illegal now, thanks to changes in the laws. Navigating all of these changes without guidance can have disastrous consequences for your financial well-being. This is why it's important to keep a tax professional on your team. A good tax advisor will stay up-to-date on developments within the tax code and will constantly be looking at ways to modify your tax strategy to make the most of these changes.

The Science of Tax Planning

The best financial planners are part detective, part scientist. We have already explored some of the ways that a tax planner is like a detective. Let's investigate how scientific methods translate very easily into financial planning:

- Like a scientist, a tax planner first identifies a problem that needs a solution. In this case, the problem is that your business is paying too much in taxes. It is the tax advisor's job to find creative solutions to that problem.

- To solve the problem, both a scientist and a tax professional would spend time gathering information about the situation. This is the part of the process when your accountant meets with you to discuss your needs and reviews your current financial situation.

- Once the information is gathered, a scientist makes a hypothesis. In the same way, a tax planner will devise a strategy that will work toward solving the problem and improving your results.

- Once the initial solution has been implemented, your tax advisor will want to follow up to determine its effectiveness. This, too, is part of the scientific process: scientists run experiments while tax planners test strategies to see which ones are the most effective.

- Based on the feedback from these initial changes, a tax planner will modify his approach and make any additional changes to continue refining results. This is a crucial step as it means the financial plan will grow and evolve over time.

Since tax planning is an ongoing process, you will probably be meeting with your tax advisor several times a year. A quarterly meeting often makes the most sense; you will have the chance to check in, explore your current financial situation, and make changes to the strategy in time to benefit by tax season.

Saving Money Is Making Money

When it comes to growing your wealth, you have two options: you can either cut your expenses or boost your profits. Either option will improve your bottom line. When you are trying to grow a business or increase your personal wealth, you need to pay attention to your options and choose the strategy that makes more sense for your situation. You may not be in a position where it is possible to raise prices or drop your overhead, for example, but you may still be able to save money by lowering your tax bill.

The fact is that most businesses pay more taxes than they need to, and they would never realize it if not for the investigation by a well-educated tax detective looking at their finances. Before you picked up this book, did you have any idea that the strategies we have discussed could be implemented? Remember that this book explains just a few of the many methods a tax coach can use to save you money.

A good tax professional, who knows the ins and outs of the tax code and can apply those rules creatively to unique situations, is an invaluable resource for any business. This could be the secret ingredient to a massive income boost.

As a business owner, identifying the best tax professional to add to your team can be a real mystery. By looking at some important clues, like that tax professional's experience within your industry and his general approach to tax planning, you can decide whether a potential accountant would be a valuable addition to your team. Being a tax detective yourself will help you determine if you have made the right choice since you will be more aware of the opportunities that exist within the tax code.

Once you have found a professional that you are comfortable with, you will be able to start discussing tactics like those found in this book and work together to create a tax strategy that will turn a profit for your business in the long haul.

Let's Review Our Clues:

- There is a difference between tax planning and tax preparation. An accountant who just prepares your taxes cannot make as much of an impact to your financial well-being as a tax advisor who can work with you to plan a financial strategy.

- Tax planning is a proactive strategy. It allows you to make smart business choices today that will affect your tax bill tomorrow.

- There is no one-size-fits-all approach to tax planning. Different industries have different requirements, and financial needs vary between individuals. It is important for a tax planner to build a financial plan around an individual's needs rather than use a cookie-cutter approach.

- A good tax advisor is like a scientist. He will constantly be experimenting and modifying his approach to ensure that your tax strategy is the best possible.

- You can outgrow your tax advisor over time, and there is no shame in getting a referral to someone who will be better suited to your situation.

- Your tax coach will become a regular part of your team, and it is worth taking the time to be sure that you get along professionally and have the same long-term goals in mind for the financial benefit of your business.

- When it comes to a business, saving money is just as good as making money. This is especially true when it comes to taxes as high earners are punished by the tax code. By trimming your taxes, you can cut down your single greatest expense as a taxpayer.

ABOUT THE AUTHOR

R. Travis Evans, MLERE, ASBC
CFP®, CAPP™, CFS®, CLA™, CWPP™, RFC®, CTC

R. Travis Evans is the founder and president of E3 Capital Designs, LLC. With over 20 years of experience counseling business owners and professionals with financial and estate planning, Travis continued to see common mistakes that were costing consumers hundreds of thousands of dollars as they transitioned into retirement. Overlooked tax savings and market losses were especially costly.

Named after his proprietary process, Economic Efficiency Engineering, Travis founded E3 Capital Designs, LLC, to help clients to not only avoid unnecessary investment risk, debt traps, and taxation, but also to capitalize on little-known planning techniques and safe opportunities for asset growth and protection—opportunities not offered through typical brokerage and banking institutions. Emphasizing wealth preservation, E-3 Capital Designs, LLC, utilizes proprietary software to verify economic strategies that maximize your financial efficiency, transforming waste and deficiency into abundant lifestyles, and secure retirements.

Since 1992, when he partnered with his father to establish Evans & Evans, Travis has garnered national recognition for his accomplishments as a consultant. In 1996, he was the youngest advisor in Texas to earn the coveted RFC designation. He is among a select group of advisors to take advanced coursework from the Wealth Preservation Institute, and he is adamant about staying current with new legislation and the ever-changing array of solutions for his clients. A Texas state rep for the Asset Protection Society, Travis has been a speaker at the

TVMA annual convention, as well as a guest lecturer in doctoral classes at Texas A&M.

Between 1986 and 1991, Travis earned his bachelor's and master's degrees while he represented Texas A&M as a scholarship athlete on both the football and rodeo teams. Widowed in 2005, Travis is the proud father of Landon and Emilie, and in 2011 he was blessed to marry Kate Toomey, a fellow Aggie and the owner of Life-In-Stride Riding Academy.

Travis can be reached at (979) 846-9476 or at travis@e3capitaldesigns.com, and you may visit Travis' website at www.e3capitaldesigns.com

CHAPTER 2

New Business 101

Tax Strategies for Freelancers and the "Forced Entrepreneur"

By Melody S. Thornton, CPA, CTC

oth of the following statements are true: small businesses are the best legal tax shelter, and self-employed people have much higher tax bills than other workers. How can such contradictory statements both be true? To solve this mystery, we will need to look at the tax strategies that can cut down the costs of your business and enable you to trim your tax bill for other sources of income as well.

What Is a Tax Shelter?

Simply put, a tax shelter is a system that allows you to minimize or avoid paying taxes. A small business fits the bill by allowing you to shift expenses from post-tax to pre-tax dollars, minimizing your total taxable income. This in effect helps reduce the taxes you pay on other sources of income.

Let's look at a simple example. Imagine that you have $100. Half of this was earned through wages at your regular office job. The other half came from an online jewelry business you run in your spare time. Imagine that 15% of that money gets taxed, leaving you with $85. However, your jewelry business has deductions that offset those taxes. You paid postage to ship the jewelry, bought packing supplies, and drove to the post office. The deductions add up to $15, offsetting the taxes and allowing you to keep the full $100 in your pocket.

This is an oversimplified example, but it shows just how helpful business deductions can be in cutting your tax costs. Since business deductions represent money you would be spending anyway, they don't cost anything extra to implement. In fact, failing to take every deduction is what causes some self-employed workers to spend far too much on taxes.

Let's look at some of the real tax strategies you can put into place right away to save money on your small business.

Setting Up a Home Business to Minimize Tax Costs

If you don't already have a business in place, there are a few things you can do while setting it up to get started on the right path. Even if your business is already established, you can make changes that will help you maximize your tax savings. When it comes to setting up a business, the two most important things you can do for your budget are to choose the correct business designation and set up your home office correctly. Let's investigate both more closely.

Choosing the Best Business Designation

A company's business designation has a major impact on the way it is taxed. You have several options to choose from when establishing a company:

- **A sole proprietorship** is the easiest business to start, but it also offers the fewest tax benefits. In a sole proprietorship, you and the business are one in the same. You pay taxes on your personal tax return and are personally liable for all business debts. You pay self-employment tax and income tax on every penny you earn.

- **A partnership** requires two or more people with interest in the company. A general partner plays an active role in the company, while a silent partner provides capital but otherwise remains uninvolved in the business's day-to-day operations. Partnerships are pass-through entities, meaning that the money earned by the business is divided among the partners, each of whom pays taxes at their personal tax rate. Like a sole proprietorship, this type of business offers few tax benefits. Unlike a sole proprietorship, a partnership can face significant non-tax pitfalls. A general partnership can be set up on a handshake or with the documents written on a napkin, and this is a recipe for disaster.

- **A C corporation** offers many tax benefits, but it is also more complex to establish and maintain than either the sole proprietorship or partnership. In C a corporation, the business is its own legal and tax entity, separate from the owner. C corporations sell ownership in the form of stock, and they pay dividends to investors. As the owner, you earn a salary, taxed as income, and dividends, taxed at the long-term capital gains tax rate.

- **An S corporation,** like a C corporation, sells ownership in the form of stock, but the income is taxed to the owners as a pass-through business, like a partnership. The tax laws that apply to the S corporation are stricter than a partnership, but the S corporation has some advantages over the partnership.

- **A Limited Liability Corporation (LLC)** can be taxed like any of the above businesses. What makes an LLC unique is that it protects the owner(s) from financial or legal liability on behalf of the company. In other words, in most cases, you won't lose personal assets to the company's debts or suits filed against it. Since LLCs are so flexible, they are a popular choice for business start-ups. However, I have been advised by attorneys that the legal protection of a Single Member LLC has not been tested in the courts; they recommend that you have at least a small-minority owner to ensure the legal protection of your personal assets.

There are benefits and drawbacks to each of these business designations, and you will need to do some research to figure out which option is the best fit for your goals. This area is one where having a professional tax and/or legal advisor can help put you on the right track. If your company is already established, it is not too late to restructure it to get the best tax benefits.

Setting Up a Home Office

Working from home comes with many lifestyle benefits, like being able to keep your dog at the office, walking into your kitchen for a snack, and working in your pajamas. It also creates some tax benefits thanks to the deductions you wall be able to claim.

Start by designating a space in your home to be the office. This doesn't need to be an entire room, but it does need to be used exclusively and regularly for business purposes. It helps if you can take some photos showing the business equipment in the area to prove that this location is set up specifically for work purposes.

Once you have a home office set up, you will be able to deduct a chunk of your living expenses every year. Regular personal expenses like your homeowner's insurance and utilities can be partially deducted as they support your business. For example, imagine that your office takes up one tenth of the total square footage of your house. You can now deduct 10 percent of your insurance and utility bills.

There are two strategies for taking this deduction. The first is to itemize exactly how much of your home is taken up by the office and apply that to your monthly expenses. The second option is simpler: you take a flat rate of $5 per square foot up to 300 square feet maximum, based on the actual square footage of your office. In some cases, the second option is better, especially if you have a large office and an overall frugal lifestyle with low utility costs. It is worth doing the math and comparing both results before claiming the deduction.

Here is another great benefit to setting up a home office that you can uncover with a bit of detective work: it allows you to deduct commuting expenses. You can normally only deduct mileage spent on business travel done after you have reached your workplace. However, if you start work at a home office and travel to a second office, your commute has been transformed into a deductible business expense. Simply waking up early and taking a few conference calls from your home office can create serious tax savings when you have a long commute each day.

However, this alone is not enough to create the home office. If this is your administrative office, you need to keep a log or calendar showing that you spend 10 hours per week working in your home office, and that you do all of your administrative work in your home office, for the convenience of your employer, if applicable.

Setting Up Your Office

Aside from the office space itself, the contents of your home office can be deducted. This is good news because setting up a home business can sometimes involve a lot of upfront costs. Keep track of everything you buy, including office supplies, packing materials, and electronics. It is best to purchase everything using the company's bank account or credit card to validate the purchases and provide a solid record of what was bought.

If you are putting your office together from items you already have in the home, you can still claim a deduction based on the actual cash value of those items. This will take some research as you will need to locate the cash value of each item you add to the office. Despite the additional hassle, this can be extremely valuable as it allows you to save money on taxes without spending anything out of your pocket.

Other Deductions

Your home office space is a major deductible expense, but it is not the only part of your business that can be used to trim your taxes. In fact, most expenses that you incur as part of doing business can be deducted if you know how to claim them. By shifting money that you are already spending into pre-tax dollars, you reduce your overall taxable income and can help offset income from sources outside of your business. Here are a few clues for finding valuable deductions:

- Be sure to deduct your mileage and automobile expenses for work-related trips. We discovered earlier that having a home office enables you to claim additional mileage, but don't forget to log all of your other work-related driving. The easiest way to keep track of your mileage is to keep a notebook or calendar in the car and update it daily with the miles driven, date, and purpose of the trip. Instead of opting for the standard mileage deduction, which is usually lower than the actual cost of fuel for most vehicles, itemize your deduction by determining the exact amount you have spent on fuel costs. Also, don't forget to account for things like oil changes and other maintenance. A percentage of these costs can be deducted as well based on the business usage of a vehicle. The IRS allows you to keep detailed records for any 90 consecutive days as long as they are a realistic sample of what your year looks like. I can't say it too many times, particularly for auto expenses: keep good records!
- Other travel expenses can also be deducted. If you have to travel in order to meet with a client, go to a networking event, or obtain additional training, be sure to deduct your travel and hotel expenses.
- Meals and entertainment can be deducted if they have a business purpose. For example, 50% of a meal can be deducted if you eat it while discussing business with a client. You must keep a copy of the receipt and include the required information; a copy of the monthly credit card statement is not acceptable documentation.

Some business owners are reluctant to take advantage of these deductions because they are afraid of audits or don't think they have the time to keep track of all of these expenses. However, skipping these deductions is a mistake. As you can see with a bit of sleuthing, maximizing your deductions can have a serious impact on your tax bill, which in effect reduces all of your business expenses. It is much easier to cut out a chunk of your biggest expenses than try to find savings by trimming an already slender budget piece by piece.

In reality, keeping track of your business deductions isn't difficult. Much of the information you need is already in your appointment book. Simply knowing who you have met with, where you were, and what the meeting was about can get you most of the way toward proper documentation. All you need to do is add up the amount spent, or you can just staple receipts to the relevant pages as you go.

You might need to adjust your habits in the beginning, especially if you are not a organized person by nature, but soon it will start to feel like second nature. The benefits of setting up this system and taking these deductions will quickly outweigh the inconvenience.

Now that we've discovered the benefits of making deductions for your home business, let's investigate how you can implement these changes without falling on the wrong side of the IRS.

Staying Compliant With the IRS

In an earlier chapter, we discovered some clues that can help you avoid audits. As long as you are following the rules, you don't have anything to fear from an audit. In most cases, taking business deductions for your company will not set you up for an audit; even if it does, the audit itself should be quick and painless as long as you have done your due diligence in maintaining records.

There are a few things you can do to audit-proof your tax return when making business deductions:

- Use accurate figures for expenses. Never round up or down; use the exact dollars and cents from your receipts. Round numbers can trigger an audit.
- Use your business bank account or credit card to make business related purchases. Avoid using your personal account for business. Even if you are a sole proprietor, it is best to set up

separate bank accounts for your personal expenses and your business in order to validate purchases.

- Take photographs or keep other types of proof on hand. For example, photograph your workspace to show that the new computer you purchased is being used there or to show the size of your office. If you hold a seminar at home, take a photograph of the colleagues there and save handouts or other materials that will prove that the meeting had a business purpose, so that you can claim food and beverage expenses.

- Have receipts to back up your deductions. You only need a receipt for expenses over $75, but it won't hurt to keep receipts for everything just to make itemizing simpler. I tell my clients to scan or copy cash register receipts since they tend to fade to nothing even before year-end, and much more so two years later when an audit arises. Electronic records are treated the same as paper records as long as they are accessible.

- Work with a tax coach to ensure you have filed correctly. Your tax coach will help you avoid pitfalls that could lead to an audit. He can also help you find additional deductions that you may not have thought about on your own.

After the first year, finding additional tax savings will get easier. Don't let fear stop you from claiming all of the deductions that you can. The guidance of a qualified tax professional will keep you in compliance with the IRS while cutting your tax bill significantly.

A Word About Profits and Losses

A home business can become a valuable tax shelter if you use business losses to offset gains in other areas. A business loss occurs whenever the profits from a business are not high enough to cover all of the businesses expenses. Most businesses see losses in their first year or two since there is a lot of overhead associated with starting up a new company. This is especially true when you are building inventory from the ground up and setting up an office space.

If your losses exceed your total other income for the year, you may have a Net Operating Loss (NOL) that you can roll backward two years and/or forward 20 years to offset income at other times. This can be very helpful in a few situations; for example, if you had high earnings and paid a lot of income tax in the two years prior to the year of your losses. Like many areas of the tax law, this is complex, and you should work with your Certified Tax Coach to see whether you can have an NOL and amount you can claim.

One thing to bear in mind while claiming your losses is that the IRS will eventually re-classify a business as a hobby if it is not profitable. This is a major problem because hobby income is taxed, but hobby expenses cannot be claimed as a deduction. Certain businesses are especially prone to being classified as hobbies since the activities are generally considered fun. Things like writing, animal showing, and selling homemade crafts can all easily slip into hobby status if you are not careful.

Fortunately, there is a way to redeem your business from the hobby classification even if you do not have profits. All you need to do is prove that the business has a profit motive. This will require you to draft a detailed business plan including profit projections and a strategy for growing the business over time. You must also be willing to change your strategy if you continue to be unprofitable; real businesses make changes if they are losing money since they are in business to make money. With your business plan in place, and your willingness to make changes as needed to prove a profit motive, your actual profits won't matter as much to the IRS.

Of course, even that strategy can't work indefinitely. It's important to discuss your options with your accountant to determine the best way to receive optimal tax benefits from your business without falling into the hobby trap.

Let's Review Our Clues:

- Small business owners can either pay more taxes than any other business or use their businesses as a smart tax shelter. The difference is in the quality of their tax planning.

- Your business designation can make a major impact on your tax strategy; take the time to research your options and make the right choice.

- Be sure to claim deductions when setting up your home business. Use your business bank account to pay for new items you buy, and keep good records of your expenses.

- You can deduct the actual cash value of your existing furniture and electronics when you use them to set up a home office.

- Meals, entertainment, and travel expenses can be deducted when they have a business purpose. You can take advantage of these deductions with minimal hassle by being organized and keeping copies of the receipts.

- You can use business losses to offset gains in other areas, but be sure that you don't end up with your business getting re-classified as a hobby after too many unprofitable years.

- Work with a Certified Tax Coach to maximize your deductions and minimize your audit risk.

ABOUT THE AUTHOR

Melody S. Thornton, CPA, CTC

Melody Thornton is a Certified Public Accountant, Certified Tax Coach, and co-author of *The Tax Detective: Uncovering the Mystery of Tax Planning*. A tax partner at CohnReznick (formerly J.H. Cohn LLP) for 20 years, Melody now uses that experience to reduce income taxes for middle-market and public companies to help small business owners, investors, and individuals claim all of the deductions and credits available to them.

Being a trusted tax advisor, who takes a holistic approach, is Melody's priority. She works closely with clients and their team of advisors (both internal and external) to explain how the tax laws impact them, so they can make the best decisions for today and the future.

Melody serves proudly on the board of directors of the Make-A-Wish Foundation of San Diego, which grants the wishes of children with life-threatening medical conditions, to enrich the human experience with hope, strength, and joy. She is a past president of the California Society of Certified Public Accountants (CalCPA), San Diego Chapter, and she serves on the CalCPA State Council, the state-level Taxation Committee of CalCPA, and the CalCPA State Board of Directors. Melody prides herself on being well connected throughout the region and state, working in collaboration with practitioners and the government, to bring the best results to her clients.

Melody can be reached at (619) 990-2832 or at msthornton.cpa@gmail.com.

www.melodycpa.com

CHAPTER 3

Is Your Business Entity Full of Tax Holes?

By Larry Farmer, CPA, CTC

I t is no surprise that the overwhelming majority of millionaires are business owners. As we have uncovered numerous tax mysteries throughout this book, a few common threads have appeared. One major clue that has come up repeatedly is the tax advantage of owning a business. When you are a business owner, you have significantly more control over your finances than you would as an employee of another company.

No matter how you make your money, there are only two ways to grow wealth: you either generate more income or cut down your spending. As an employee, your options are limited. You can work overtime or trim your personal budget, but you probably won't be able to make a dramatic difference doing either. As a business owner, however, you have more control over how much you earn. You can modify your business strategies to boost profits, and you can cut down operating costs significantly. Most importantly, you can take advantage of tax opportunities and loopholes to trim your company's tax liability.

Why Do Businesses Get So Many Benefits?

What Difference Does Business Entity Form Make?

In the eyes of the government, businesses are unique legal entities. For the most part, a company is considered separate from its owner or founder. This is why companies can take on a life of their own: even after the founder dies, the business lives on, passing through generations, and growing its own financial legacy. Since businesses are their own legal entities, they are taxed differently from individuals.

There are several types of business forms and each one has its own benefits and drawbacks from a tax perspective. Two people with exactly the same type of business and income can earn vastly different amounts of money depending on how their businesses are structured.

For example, imagine that you own a restaurant. After all of your expenses have been accounted for, you brought in $100,000 in profits for the year. If you ran that restaurant as a sole proprietorship, you would pay self-employment tax on 100% of the money you earned. This would be added to your regular income tax. The net self-employment tax in this example is currently 13.3% of $100,000, for a total of $13,300 paid to the IRS.

If you restructured the business as an S corporation, you could possibly reduce your self-employment taxes. This is because the owner of an S corporation pays himself a reasonable salary, just as he would any other employee. Any remaining profits are distributed to him, and these distributions are not subject to self-employment taxes. Therefore, as the owner of this hypothetical restaurant, you could give yourself a $50,000 annual salary (if reasonable compensation), and the other $50,000 would pass through to you as distributions. In this case, you would pay half as much self-employment tax as you did as a sole proprietor—effectively putting $6,650 back into your pocket.

My long-time client Fred Entrepreneur has been self-employed for more than ten years. Fred's self-employment income has averaged $200,000 per year. Over the last decade, I have tried to persuade Fred to use tax planning to reduce his tax liability. I have heard countless excuses: he is too busy to meet with me, he thinks it will be too much trouble to implement a tax plan, etc.

I calculated that if he had selected the proper entity ten years ago and employed tax planning techniques that would require little if any additional effort on his part, he would have saved over $20,000 in taxes each year—a total of $200,000!

With that in mind, let's investigate your business form options in detail, so that we can solve the mystery of which option is best for your needs.

Basic Entity Choices

Your business entity choice primarily affects two things: the way the company's profits will be taxed, and the amount of liability an owner carries. Some business entities are easier to set up than others, and you may want the feedback of both an attorney and a tax expert when establishing a company. This will help to ensure that you are making the best choice for your specific needs as there are benefits and drawbacks to each company structure.

Sole Proprietorship

A sole proprietorship is the easiest type of business to form because it requires little in the way of formal paperwork. If you choose to work under a pseudonym, you may need to register the fictitious name as a "DBA" in your county. Depending on the type of business you are running, you may need to obtain a business license. Otherwise, setting up a sole proprietorship can be as simple as hanging out a shingle and doing business. There is no formal paperwork needed to establish a business entity because, in the eyes of the government, there is no separate business entity: you and your company are one and the same.

A sole proprietor can hire employees, but he retains sole ownership of his business. From a tax perspective, all business profits are treated as personal income, and sole proprietorship taxes are filed on the owner's personal tax return. The business owner is also personally liable for the company's debts as well as litigation raised against the business. In other words, if you are a freelance journalist working as a sole proprietor, you can be personally sued for libel for the things you write; if you are a journalist working for a company, the company itself is liable. There are exceptions to this, and the applicable laws can vary, so a consultation with an attorney is important. Aside from their ease of creation, sole proprietorships offer few tax benefits. Sole proprietors pay more in taxes than other types of business owners because 100% of the company's profits are subject to both income and self-employment taxes.

Pros:

- Simplest business to set up.
- Minimal operating costs.
- Few start-up and administrative expenses.

Cons:

- The only liability protection you have comes from buying business insurance.
- You pay both income and self-employment tax.
- You will face a higher audit risk than other businesses.

Partnership

A partnership is essentially a combination of sole proprietors. Whenever you start a business with one or more other people, it is automatically considered a partnership, whether or not you draft any partnership agreements. Of course, it is in your best interests to speak with an attorney and file some paperwork to precisely define the parameters of the partnership. Otherwise, you may find yourself personally liable for the actions and debts of your partner.

In terms of taxes, a partnership is a pass-through entity. This means that all profits are divided among the owners, each of whom pays income and self-employment taxes. Like a sole proprietorship, partnerships offer few tax benefits because of this. They do have the benefit of spreading liability out among two or more people, which can help soften the blow of business debts.

Pros:

- You will have relatively low start-up costs.
- Little required paperwork to form the company.
- If there are business debts, you share the liability with your partner(s).

Cons:

- Sharing a business can be challenging, especially if you don't have solid agreements set up in the beginning.
- You pay both income and self-employment taxes on 100% of your share of the profits if you actively participate in the business.
- Sharing liability can also have negative consequences, since you are responsible for the actions of your partner(s).

Corporation

A corporation is very different from a partnership or a sole proprietorship. Corporations are their own legal entities. They have their own debts, and taxes are filed independently of the owner. Corporations can be passed down easily from one owner to the next, and in many cases, ownership is actually divided among multiple investors through the sale of shares.

When you own a share of a company, you hold partial ownership of that company. The dividends that you receive as a shareholder are actually residual profits left over after wages and expenses have been paid. While you're probably most familiar with shares for companies that are publicly traded, privately held companies can sell shares as well, allowing ownership of the business to be spread across multiple shareholders without the personal liability risks inherent in a partnership.

Setting up a corporation is more expensive and time-consuming than other types of businesses, but corporations also have more available benefits. There are multiple types of corporations, and each one has its own unique features. Let's dig deeper, and see which corporation offers the most tax benefits.

C Corporation

A C corporation is the standard or "default" corporate structure for most major businesses. If you own corporate stock, it is almost certainly from a C corp. The vast majority of major corporations are C corps because there are no limits to ownership: a C corporation can have as many stockholders as are willing to buy shares in the company.

From a financial perspective, C corporations have many benefits: the corporation is a separate legal and tax entity, so it has its own tax return and its own deductible expenses. The company's owner is just like any other shareholder, although he probably owns more shares than other investors do. As the owner of a C corporation, you pay yourself a salary just as you would pay all of your other employees, and those wages would be deductible on the corporation's taxes.

After all expenses are deducted, the corporation pays taxes based on corporate rates. The remaining money passes through to shareholders as dividends. All shareholders pay tax on those dividends, and all employees—including the owner—pay income tax.

C corporations are your best choice if you ever plan to go public with the company and have its stock traded through the New York Stock Exchange. If you plan to keep the business small, a C corporation might not be the best bet due to how complicated they can be to establish and run. However, it is worth investigating your options and discussing them with both an attorney and a tax professional to see if a C corporation would be a good fit for your needs and goals.

Pros:
- You can have as many shareholders as you want.
- The owner doesn't share liability with the company.
- You have multiple deductible fringe benefits available to claim.

Cons:

- The start-up costs for establishing a C corporation can be high.
- The administrative costs of establishing and running the business are high.
- You can end up being taxed twice if you receive wages and hold stock.

S Corporation

An S corporation is better suited to small, privately held businesses. Unlike a C corporation, which can have unlimited shareholders, S corporations are limited to a maximum of 100 shareholders. Additionally, whereas C corporation stock can be held by other corporations and other nonperson entities, S corporation shares generally must be held by individuals.

What makes an S corporation attractive is the way that distributions are handled. As with a C corporation, the owner of an S corporation pays himself a salary. Remaining profits are distributed to shareholders. In an S corporation, these distributions are not subject to self-employment tax. If you recall the example at the beginning of this chapter, this means that you could cut your self-employment tax significantly. Saving shareholders from double taxation is the primary benefit of an S corporation over a C corporation.

Pros:

- You don't share liability with your company.
- Your self-employment taxes are minimized.
- There is no double taxation for shareholders.

Cons:

- You will have high start-up costs and administrative expenses.
- You can only have 100 shareholders.
- You may not have quite as many deductible expenses and fringe benefits as a C corporation.

LLC

LLC stands for "limited liability company," and this name makes the primary benefit of this business designation clear. When you own an LLC, you are separate from the company in terms of your financial and legal liability. The unique thing about an LLC is that it can be established for a business of any size, and it can be taxed as any of the above types of business forms.

In other words, an LLC can have one employee or a thousand, and its tax strategy can change over time to keep up with the needs of the business. You can establish your sole proprietorship as an LLC today and enjoy limited liability benefits immediately while still being taxed as a sole proprietor. As the business grows, you can change your LLC to be taxed like an S corporation, reaping the financial benefits of that strategy.

Thanks to their flexibility, LLCs are very popular choices for start-up companies. They do have some weaknesses, so they are not always the perfect option, but they are often the best choice for a new company that has yet to establish itself. To set up an LLC, you will need to consult with an attorney about filling out the appropriate paperwork.

<u>Pros:</u>
- Owners carry limited liability.
- The business' tax structure is flexible.
- An LLC is fairly easy to establish and can be formed with just one employee.

<u>Cons:</u>
- The liability protection is not perfect, especially for single-owner companies.
- An LLC takes more effort to form than a sole proprietorship or partnership, since you will need the help of an attorney.
- There are no inherent tax benefits to an LLC beyond those offered by other types of businesses.

Getting the Best Start

As you can see, there are pros and cons to every type of business entity, so there is no simple answer to the question, "Which business entity is best?" You need to carefully consider your needs as a business owner and investigate your options with professionals, taking into account both tax and liability considerations.

You may find that the tax benefits of a particular business structure are not worth the start-up and administrative expenses of the business. It may be worthwhile to keep your company as a sole proprietorship or partnership until it grows, and then restructure it once your income and expenses rise. On the other hand, it might be best to form an LLC now and take advantage of its flexibility. All of these options are viable in different situations, and a Certified Tax Coach can help you make the right decision.

Let's Review the Results of Our Investigation:

- Businesses offer a legal tax shelter that allows business owners to grow wealth more efficiently than people who work for others.

- Tax benefits are purposely written into the tax code to reward business owners.

- Choosing the right business entity is a crucial step in developing a smart tax strategy.

- Sole proprietorships and partnerships are the easiest businesses to start, but they offer the fewest tax benefits.

- Corporations offer more tax benefits but are more complex to establish.

- A corporation is its own separate legal entity and pays its own taxes.

- In a C corporation, you can have unlimited shareholders, and you pay taxes on both your salary and your dividends.

- In an S corporation, you avoid paying self-employment taxes on distributions, but you lose some of the other benefits of a C corporation.
- An LLC is a popular choice for start-ups due to its flexibility.
- Ultimately, you will want to research your options and discuss them with a tax consultant and an attorney to ensure you are making the best choice.

One more thing: in the course of business, especially in the service industry, it is important for the client to feel his concerns and questions are being addressed. You can accomplish this in a variety of ways through active listening techniques, a relaxed physical environment, and by making use of visual aids. Everyone has a learning style that works best for them. When asked, a common response from many people will be that they consider themselves visual learners. So the phrase, "a picture is worth a thousand words" is worth considering when detailing the different types of business entities. I have found that one of the most effective ways of presenting the potentially confusing details of choosing the most beneficial entity structure within a tax plan is by providing the client with a detailed flow chart.

The flow charts I provide to my clients have ranged from the very simple, providing information on three or four different entities, to an extreme array of colors, shapes, lines, and arrows that lay out the complicated ownership and income flows amongst 20 different businesses and individuals. I have the pleasure in most instances of seeing my clients' immediate understanding when I present them with a picture that shows how choosing the right type of business structure can benefit them and result in tax savings for the future. Beyond that, it is always of equal enjoyment to see the smiles and hear the comment, "This is so pretty!"

Pretty or not, remember that good planning is essential to minimizing your taxes. When you are a good tax detective and seek help from the right professionals, you will reap the benefits of the best structure for you. When you minimize your taxes, you maximize your profits!

ABOUT THE AUTHOR

R. Larry Farmer, CPA, CTC

R. Larry Farmer is a CPA and Certified Tax Coach, as well as the founding principal of R. Larry Farmer, P.C., since 2005. Co-author of the 2012 best seller *Tax Breaks of the Rich and Famous*, Larry has been a leader in public accounting for over 25 years. Not your typical "glorified historian" accountant, Larry loves to add innovation and creativity to the tired, old ways traditional accountants do things. He has a passion for helping small businesses that are usually under-served. Larry's favorite area of work is proactive tax planning. His firm provides full-service tax preparation and accounting service to support the proactive tax plan that is delivered.

Larry is a Certified Public Accountant licensed in Texas. He holds a Bachelor of Administration in Finance from Texas A&M University. He has had a rich and varied career. Formerly, he was US tax manager at Electronic Data Systems Corporation (EDS), and prior to that he was an internal revenue agent for the IRS. These experiences allow Larry to see transactions from the viewpoint of individuals, corporations, and the government.

Because Larry emphasizes staying current on the latest developments in tax law, he is a member of many professional organizations, including the American Institute of Certified Public Accountants, the Texas Society of Certified Public Accountants, the National Society of Accountants, and the National Association of Tax Professionals.

Larry has been chosen for the prestigious Best in Dallas/Ft. Worth in Taxation award by *Texas Monthly* magazine and voted the Best Accountant/CPA Readers Choice in both 2011 and 2012.

Larry has served his community in Rotary for over ten years. He is the husband of Lynette (a retired pre-school teacher), the proud father of two adult children, and grandfather to three. Larry enjoys sports, reading about history, and traveling—and, most of all, his family.

Regardless of where you are located, for more information about Larry Farmer's services, or to set up an appointment, visit his website at www.cpataxteam.com, or give him a call at (972) 596-2005.

CHAPTER 4

The Hidden Theft

Stop letting the IRS take more than their share of your money by deducting the fun things in life

by Damon Yudichak, MBA, CPA

Some mysteries of the tax code are easily cracked by anyone with some financial-planning experience. Others, however, are hidden more deeply. There are some deductions that even your accountant may miss because he or she is unaware of them or simply does not think they apply to you. Overlooking these deductions can have a major impact on your tax bill, and it is worth finding a financial advisor who can help you squeeze as much value from your tax strategy as possible.

Why is it that some tax strategies remain a mystery even to tax professionals? In most cases, it is because accountants are caught in a routine and rarely deviate from it. Many people think of their tax coaches simply as people who file taxes at the end of the year, but this outlook ignores the greater value of tax planning as a way to develop sound financial strategies for your home and business.

Throughout this book, we have discovered many valuable clues to building a solid financial strategy through smart tax planning. In this chapter, let's dig deeper into the tax mystery to uncover some of the clues that even your current financial planner may have overlooked.

Investigating Tax Deductions

The tax code is written with a number of built-in loopholes that can be utilized by people who know what they are doing. Taking advantage of these loopholes and opportunities is legal as long as you do it correctly. In fact, the loopholes exist specifically so that people can benefit from them.

In general, the point of deductions and tax breaks is to reward certain behaviors, particularly those of small businesses. Since small businesses provide a valuable service to the community in the form of job creation, it is in the IRS's best interest to reward small-business owners through tax breaks that can lower the barrier of entry. Similarly, offering tax incentives to employers who offer benefits to their workers encourages those businesses to provide these benefits, which in turn helps the workers as well.

With that in mind, it is important to remember that not every person will be able to benefit from every tax break and deduction. Before taking a deduction, it is important to understand how the tax law applies to your specific situation, and you should seek the assistance of a Certified Tax Coach to help you understand these laws. By knowing the basics, you will be able to ask the right questions to receive the guidance you need.

Money You Were Already Spending

We have talked already about the value of spending pre-tax dollars by using deductions. In this chapter, we will look more closely at some deductions that you can take for activities that you are already doing. By finding ways to deduct the "fun" activities in your life, you can free up more money in your budget to put toward savings, investments, or daily necessities.

In order to make these tax strategies work, you will need to identify the places where you are already spending money and find a way to deduct those expenses. Buying something that you don't need, just so you can deduct it on your tax return, is probably not a smart financial strategy. Finding a way to categorize your purchases, so that they can be deducted, however, can save you a lot of money.

Let's investigate a few ways that you can turn regular activities into tax-reducing opportunities.

Business Expenses

We discovered earlier that businesses can be a great tax shelter thanks to the deductions available to small-business owners. We have already touched on a few of those benefits, such as deducting the cost of a home office and vehicle maintenance expenses when the car is used for business.

If you haven't already set up a home office, you are missing out on one of the most valuable opportunities for trimming your tax bill. You are already paying your mortgage and utilities and by shifting a portion of those expenses into a tax-deductible category, you can effectively trim your monthly budget.

Other tax-saving opportunities are not as obvious. Here are a few lesser-known business deductions that you may be able to apply to your own company:

- When establishing a new business, you can deduct up to $10,000 for start-up costs associated with creating that business. These costs might include things like computers for an office or kitchen equipment for a restaurant. If you spend more than $10,000, you can roll the additional expense forward to deduct in future years. However, if you choose to do this, there are some limitations: the value of your deduction will reduce by one dollar for every dollar over $60,000 that you spend.

- When you purchase items for your new business, you can choose to depreciate them all at once and claim that depreciation rather than waiting for them to depreciate over time. This works only when taken during the first year of a new business, and it only applies to new items that you have purchased yourself. This is called the "Section 179" deduction after the part of the tax code that allows it to be taken.

- When buying a new work vehicle, the type of automobile you purchase will affect the amount you can deduct. The standard deduction for a car is $11,060. If the vehicle weighs more than 6,000 pounds, however, it is classified as a "heavy vehicle," and these can be deducted at $25,000. Many large SUVs and pickups will meet this requirement.

- Annual costs for advertising and promoting your business can be deducted. Among these expenses are your business cards, webhosting costs, advertisements, etc.

- Ongoing training and research about your business can also be deducted. For example, you can deduct costs associated with business seminars and conventions. You can also deduct the cost of books related to your trade, trade magazine subscriptions, and the dues to professional clubs and organizations.

- Gym equipment, including a swimming pool, can be deducted as a business expense under certain circumstances. If you have employees—including yourself, if you own a corporation—and those employees regularly use your fitness equipment, the maintenance costs of that equipment are tax deductible under Section 132(j)(4) of the tax code.

These are just a few of the business expenses that can be deductible. Any ongoing expense related to the maintenance of your company can qualify for a deduction. Some creativity will help you and your tax advisor identify the opportunities that make sense for your specific situation.

Hire Your Family

If you own a business, one of the smartest moves you can make might be hiring family members. Since you are already providing for your spouse or children financially, shifting some of that assistance into wages and benefits can provide you with a much-needed tax break.

Consider this: if you are already putting money aside for your spouse's retirement, wouldn't it be better to receive a tax credit for establishing an IRA? Similarly, doesn't it make more sense to pay your son wages for work he can do to help the business, allowing him to receive untaxed income toward a college fund, rather than to simply set aside that money after tax?

There are many opportunities to hire a family member to work in your business, and most bring valuable tax incentives. We investigated many of these in earlier chapters, but here are a few lesser-known opportunities for writing off employee expenses:

- You can offer a "length of service" award to any employee who has worked for you longer than five years. This award can be given out indefinitely at five-year intervals. To qualify, the award must be non-cash and have a value of $400 or less. As long as it meets these criteria, the expense is wholly deductible.

- If you provide snacks or refreshments to your employees, you can deduct some of those expenses as long as they are reasonable. Additionally, you can deduct the cost of an occasional dinner for your employees for a special occasion, such as when they are staying late or working over a holiday.

- If you give birthday or holiday gifts to your employees, you can deduct the cost. To qualify, the expense must be less than $25, and it must be non-cash. You can get around the cash rule by offering a gift card.

- Similarly, other gifts for your employees, such as greeting cards for a worker who has recently had a baby, or sympathy flowers can be deducted as long as their cash value is below $25.

All of these deductions are available to every employee in your business. This is even true of your family members as long as they are bona fide employees. In other words, this rule allows you to deduct $25 of your child's birthday presents every year as long as he works for the family business.

In order to make this work, you will need to provide proof that your family member is a bona fide employee of your company. You will also need to show that he or she is being paid wages that are appropriate for the work being done. This means keeping good records and, where appropriate, creating W-2s for wages, but the benefits can far outweigh the hassles.

Entertainment

The most valuable tax strategies are those that allow you to enjoy pleasurable activities while spending pre-tax dollars. It comes as a surprise to many people that quite a few hobbies and interests can be deducted as long as those activities are coupled with a business purpose. Since many business owners often find their work and personal lives deeply entwined, such opportunities arise more frequently than you might expect.

For example, you can deduct 50% of meal expenses when you discuss business before, during, or after the meal. If you were going to eat lunch at a restaurant or pick up a cup of coffee anyway, consider inviting a colleague along and discuss business matters while you wait. Schedule client meetings to coincide with your usual lunch break, so that you can deduct part of the meal you would be eating anyway. These are small expenses, but they can quickly add up over the course of a year.

Another opportunity arises when you look at hobby activities. We discovered earlier that a hobby cannot usually be deducted on your taxes. However, there are a few ways to turn your hobby into a business-related activity, creating many tax-saving opportunities:

- Turn your hobby into a business. As long as you have a profit motive and plan laid out for the business, you can prevent it from being classified as a hobby by the IRS. Take the time to draft up a business plan and some financial projections to prove the legitimacy of your endeavor. If your hobby happens to turn a profit, you can enjoy some added income while participating in an activity that you enjoy.

- If your hobby is social in nature, brainstorm some ways to add a business purpose to it. For example, you might invite a client with you on a golfing trip, so that you can discuss business and thus deduct some of the golfing expenses.

- Think outside the box. For example, if your child is involved in sports, see if you could sponsor the team by putting your business logo on the jersey. This turns the sporting event into a marketing event, allowing you to deduct some of the expenses associated with traveling to games.

Another area with plenty of available deductions is travel expenses. When you travel for work, you are able to deduct things like gas, hotel stays, and meals away from home. In some cases, these deductions can be extended to your family if they come with you. This means that you can easily convert a business trip into a family vacation. By simply balancing your business obligations with a few fun family activities, you can squeeze extra value out of the trip and make it more enjoyable while trimming your expenses.

In order to claim these expenses, you will need to be careful about documenting the business purpose of the trip and keeping the costs reasonable. This is one area where you should be sure to discuss your options with a tax professional, as people often try to deduct travel and meal expenses incorrectly. Save yourself the hassle of an audit by doing your research in advance and planning the trip accordingly.

Renting Out Your Home

Here is one well-guarded secret that most people are unaware of: you can enjoy tax-free income from the rental of your home. This opportunity is available to any homeowner who rents out a portion of the home for fewer than 15 days out of the year. There are no tax deductions associated with rental expenses, but the income you bring in from this home rental is tax-free. Used wisely, this can be very powerful.

For example, if you live in a large city, there is probably at least one major event each year. Sporting events, concerts, cultural events, and conventions are all likely contenders. During that time of year, many people will flock to the area and may have a hard time finding accommodations. Rent out a room in your home for the weekend and advertise it to the people attending the event. Since there will be so much demand, you will be able to charge quite handsomely, and all of that money will go directly into your pocket.

You don't have to use your personal home for this purpose, either. If you own a motor home, vacation home, or any other residential property, you can rent it out for up to 15 days out of the year without incurring any income tax on the rental income.

Finding More Opportunities

As we have discovered repeatedly through our detective work, the tax code is complex and full of opportunities. The ideas listed here represent just a small portion of what you may be able to incorporate into your own tax plan. Depending on your situation, you may be able to deduct many things not listed here.

There is one thing to bear in mind as you search for these deductions: there is no one-size-fits-all approach to tax planning. Deductions that work perfectly for one business will not work for another and might even be illegal under different circumstances.

Just as you would never solve a mystery without uncovering all of the clues, you shouldn't make a tax plan based on incomplete information. Use these ideas as a starting point for your conversation with your tax planner, so that together you can create a customized financial strategy.

Let's Review Our Clues:

- Many tax professionals are unaware of all the available deductions or simply don't take the time to find opportunities for their clients.

- Some of the most valuable deductions allow you to shift your purchases from post-tax to pre-tax dollars.

- When setting up a business, you can claim a few lesser-known deductions, including start-up costs and work vehicle acquisition.

- Hiring family members is one powerful way to maximize the value of employee tax deductions. Since you are already spending money to support your family, using wages as a vehicle for that money offers tax advantages.

- Aside from obvious deductions, like health insurance and retirement plans, many employee expenses can be deducted. Some of these expenses are only deductible if they are non-cash, but you can circumvent this issue by offering gift cards instead for things like employee recognition awards.

- A bit of planning can turn your hobbies and leisure activities into tax-deductible business activities. This includes things like meals, travel expenses, and even family vacations if they are planned carefully.

- Homeowners can rent out their properties for up to 15 days out of the year without incurring tax on the rental income.

- There is no one-size-fits-all tax approach, so be sure to discuss your situation with a Certified Tax Coach to be sure that your financial strategy is audit-proof and matches your needs.

ABOUT THE AUTHOR

Damon Yudichak, MBA, CPA

As a Certified Tax Coach, Damon works with business owners to reduce their liabilities and increase their tax savings. He considers his three-year commitment to the US Army to be one of the best decisions he has made as it formed the backbone of his work ethic. Damon's mission is to help business owners find money they didn't know they had.

Damon purchased his first business, a commercial cleaning business, while studying accounting at North Carolina State University. While running this business, he learned firsthand the joys and challenges of business ownership. It was also there that he received his first big tax bill.

After receiving his accounting degree from NC State, Damon worked as a corporate accountant, tax accountant, and auditor. He went on to earn a Master's of Business Administration in order to broaden his business understanding beyond tax and accounting. The most valuable lesson he learned from business school is that *all* business is based on personal relationships.

In 2010, the *Triangle Business Journal* awarded Damon with the 40 Under 40 Leadership Award.

In his free time, Damon enjoys spending time with his wife, two daughters, and son. He enjoys running and training for marathons. He loves the adventure that marathons bring into his life.

Damon can be reached at (919) 926-1342 or at damon@yudichakcpa.com and you may visit his website at www.yudichakcpa.com.

CHAPTER 5

The Secret in The Attic

*What You Don't Know
about the Affordable Care Act
Will Cost You Thousands*

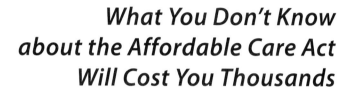

By Clinton Robinson, CTC

ince this book is *The Tax Detective,* let's start with a mystery: what do health insurance laws have to do with tax strategy? These days, health insurance affects your tax bill a lot more than you'd think, thanks to the Affordable Care Act (ACA), also known as Obamacare. This cluster of laws first passed in 2010, but the bulk of its changes didn't go into effect until 2014, and it will continue to roll out in stages until 2016.

The new healthcare law affects individuals and small businesses, bringing with it a mixed bag of benefits and drawbacks. The law has been quite controversial since it was first proposed, with plenty of confusing and even untrue claims being made by people from both sides of political party lines. This has led to a lot of confusion among individuals about what the law really does, and how it affects them.

In this chapter, let's investigate the ACA, and see if we can find some clues about how it affects you.

What Is the Affordable Care Act?

Before we can look at ways the Affordable Care Act affects your taxes and financial strategy, you have to understand what it actually is. Simply put, the ACA is a bundle of laws governing the way health insurance is bought and sold in the US. Here are a few highlights:

- People can no longer be turned down for insurance due to pre-existing medical conditions.
- Children can remain on their parents' insurance policy until age 26.
- People receiving Medicare Part D can receive discounts on certain prescription drugs to make up for gaps in prescription drug coverage.
- Insurance companies must put the bulk of their premiums toward maintaining and improving policies: 80% of individual policy premiums and 85% of group policy premiums must be earmarked for that purpose.
- Plans can no longer include lifetime or annual limits.
- In some states, Medicaid has been expanded to offer insurance to adults living near the poverty line.

Thanks to the ACA, insurance policies are standardized between companies. Every insurer must now offer bronze-, silver-, gold-, and platinum-level policies, with each tier covering a specific amount of medical expenses. Policies must also include full coverage for certain types of preventative care, including women's health exams and some vaccines. A low-cost catastrophic health plan, which is designed for major accidents or illnesses and covers just a handful of doctor's visits per year, is available to people under the age of 30.

Customers can compare and purchase policies through a "health insurance exchange," a website that facilitates the research and sale of insurance. The government portal for these exchanges is Healthcare.gov, and many states have established their own sites. Bear in mind that the exchange is not a healthcare provider itself, and Obamacare is not an insurance company. The exchange just gets you in contact with participating insurance companies.

It's still possible to buy insurance individually through any private health insurance provider, and existing policies have only been canceled or changed if they did not meet the standards set by the ACA. This means that, for many people who already had health insurance, the ACA's changes may not have been noticeable.

If this was where the story ended, Obamacare would not be nearly as controversial as it is. It also wouldn't warrant its own chapter in a tax accounting book. Let's dig a little deeper into the mystery to see how it all fits together.

Understanding How Obamacare Affects Taxes

The underlying purpose of the Affordable Care Act is to reduce the number of uninsured Americans and remove some of the boundaries that people would encounter when trying to purchase insurance. Nationwide, around 17% of Americans were uninsured prior to the passing of the ACA. Many of those with insurance had bare-bones policies that did not cover all necessary medical expenses or had prohibitively high deductibles that essentially rendered the insurance useless. To counteract this problem, insurance had to become affordable and accessible for everyone. This meant making an individual insurance mandate requiring everyone to carry insurance. Without the mandate, the theory goes, only sick people would buy insurance, and insurers could no longer profit from their policies. Only by spreading risk across the pool of young, healthy people could it be possible to offer affordable coverage to old and sick people.

This is where the tax connection comes into play: people who choose not to carry insurance (and are not exempt due to financial hardship) will have to pay a tax penalty at the end of the year. In 2014, the penalty is small to allow people time to get used to the new law. By 2016, however, it will be a rather formidable fee:

- In 2014, the penalty is $95 per adult and $47.50 per child, up to a maximum of $285 per family or 1% of the family's income, whichever is lower.

- In 2015, this will go up to $325 per adult and $162.50 per child, up to a maximum of $975 per family or 2% of a family's income, whichever is lower.
- In 2016, the fee will cap at $695 per adult and $347.50 per child, up to $2,085 or 2.5% of a family's income, whichever is lower.
- Beyond 2016, the penalty for all future increases will be tied to inflation.

So, as an individual, you have two options: you can either pay for insurance, or you can opt and pay the tax penalty. If you opt to buy insurance, you may qualify for government assistance. People with incomes below 400% of the Federal Poverty Limit will receive a tax subsidy to help cover the cost of insurance. The lower your income, the more help you'll receive. You can see how much of a subsidy you'll qualify for at the Kaiser Family Foundation's website: http://kff.org/interactive/subsidy-calculator.

Additionally, people with incomes below 133% of the poverty line can qualify for Medicaid in several states. Not every state has opted to expand Medicaid, but low-income individuals are exempt from the tax penalty if the total cost of health insurance would be more than 8% of their total income. You can see which states have expanded Medicaid, and which are in the process of doing so, at Kaiser's website as well: http://kff.org/health-reform/state-indicator/state-activity-around-ex-panding-medicaid-under-the-affordable-care-act/.

If you opt out of buying insurance, you face the tax penalty. However, this penalty is not applied like other taxes. You cannot be sent to collections or jailed for failure to pay this tax. Instead, the amount of the penalty will be withheld from your current or future tax returns. Therefore, smart management of your tax withholdings can effectively prevent the penalty from affecting you. This is definitely a strategy to discuss with your Certified Tax Coach.

Other Important Changes

The individual insurance mandate and related tax penalty are not the only link between the ACA and taxes. Here are a few other changes that can affect your tax planning:

- The floor for tax deductions on medical expenses has gone up to 10%.

- Earned and investment income over $200,000 is now subject to a 3.8% Medicare tax.

- Because insurance policies are standardized, high-deductible plans are not always available to individuals, so you may not be able to use an HSA.

- Contributions to flexible spending accounts are capped at $2,500 per year.

As a keen detective will notice, some of these changes have a greater effect on high-income individuals. The tax on investment income is particularly important as investment income was previously not subject to Medicare tax. Although 3.8% is not a sizable figure, it can add up. Later, we'll look at some strategies for avoiding the worst of this tax.

If you're a small-business owner, you will face some additional considerations as well:

- All companies with more than 50 full-time employees must provide insurance coverage to those workers.

- Businesses with more than 250 employees must show the aggregate value of the health coverage they provide to ensure that it is sufficient.

- Businesses with fewer than 25 employees do not need to offer insurance, but they can utilize a 35% tax credit to offset the cost of coverage if they do opt to provide benefits.

Like individuals, businesses also face tax penalties if they fail to adhere to these guidelines. The tax penalty for a business is $2,000 per employee over the first 50. This means that if you have 52 employees, you would only pay a penalty for two of them. Depending on the size of your company, you might prefer to take the penalty rather than offer insurance.

We'll investigate this and other money-saving strategies in a moment. First, let's take a look at the real-world effect of this law on people's finances.

Is Health Insurance Cheaper Now?

At the time of writing, 2014 is winding down, and we've had some time to see the ACA in action. So far, it's been off to a rocky start, due in part to political resistance. Some states have refused to fully participate, either by failing to set up an insurance exchange, denying Medicaid expansion, or both.

Additionally, the insurance exchanges often have few participating companies, reducing the amount of competition that could drive down rates. Finally, the standardization of insurance means that many bare-bones policies are no longer viable, forcing the people who carried them to upgrade to more thorough coverage.

For many people, all of this means that health insurance actually costs more today than it did prior to the ACA. The price difference varies between states, and overall the average cost of insurance is lower than might be expected. Health insurance costs have traditionally gone up from one year to the next. Although insurance costs more in 2014 than in 2013, the increase was less than year-to-year increases prior to the ACA. This suggests that Obamacare really is cutting the cost of insurance, even if it's not a dramatic or widespread change. For information on how Obamacare affects health insurance costs in your state, visit: http://www.newrepublic.com/article/118966/obamacare-premiums-2015-no-rate-shock-just-modest-increases.

Smart Tax Strategies

So far, we've uncovered what Obamacare is, and how it affects you as a taxpayer and business owner. We've looked at what changes the law makes to health insurance and tax penalties that go hand in hand with those changes. But the mystery is not solved just yet. Before we can call this case closed, we'll need to figure out how you can modify your own tax strategy to get the most out of the ACA while keeping more of your own money in your pocket.

For Individuals

As an individual, your first concern is avoiding the tax penalty. If you have health insurance through your employer, you don't need to worry about this; you will not face penalties at the end of the year. This is also true for anyone who continues to carry an individual insurance policy. If you're currently uninsured and on the fence about obtaining insurance, here are a few things to consider:

- **Is your income within 133 of the poverty level?** If so, you may qualify for Medicaid. Check the eligibility guidelines on the Medicaid website: http://www.medicaid.gov/AffordableCare-Act/Provisions/Eligibility.html

- **Is your income within 400% of the poverty line?** If so, you'll qualify for some financial assistance in paying your insurance premiums. Use the subsidy calculator from the Kaiser Family Foundation to check the amount of your subsidy: http://kff.org/wp-content/themes/vip/kff/static/subsidy-calculator-widget.html

- **Are you under age 26?** If so, you can use your parents' insurance, which may be cheaper than buying your own.

- **Are you under 30 and in good health?** If so, a catastrophic health insurance plan would be cheaper than a traditional policy, and may be enough to meet your needs.

- **Is the average cost of insurance in your area more than 9.5% of your annual income?** If so, you are exempt from the tax penalty.

If you are still considering going without health insurance, remember what I said earlier: the tax penalty is not collected the same way as other taxes. If you modify your tax withholdings, so that you never expect a return, the tax penalty will not affect you. This may change in the future, so be sure to pay attention to the law and follow the lead of your Certified Tax Coach on this choice.

Aside from avoiding tax penalties for going without insurance, high earning individuals and those with investment income must make a strategy for escaping the new Medicare tax. The easiest way to do this is to shift your investments to tax-free or tax-deferred vehicles like an IRA or municipal bond. Talk with your tax coach about investment options to see what makes the most sense for your needs.

For the Self-Employed

If you're self-employed, you'll have the same considerations as any other taxpayer when it comes to buying insurance. The ACA has made affordable health insurance possible for many freelancers and entrepreneurs who otherwise had difficulty finding coverage, so you may find that you greatly benefit from the new law.

However, some people have found the opposite to be true: individuals who already carried bare-bones, affordable healthcare plans prior to the ACA have found those plans canceled or replaced with more expensive options that meet the standards established by the ACA. This means that your insurance bill may be higher than it was in the past, but a tax subsidy should help to offset the cost.

Qualifying for a tax subsidy as a self-employed individual can be difficult as many freelancers have income that fluctuates. Your subsidy will be based on last year's tax return, not your current earnings. This means that if you had an unusually high income last year or have uneven earnings spread across several months of work, you may face some challenges in paying for your insurance. The best way to offset this is through financial planning and budgeting of your income to smooth over the peaks and valleys you encounter throughout the year.

Also remember that, as a self-employed worker, you can claim your health insurance costs as a business expense on your itemized tax deduction. You cannot, however, write off the tax penalty, so it's generally in your best interests to buy insurance.

Another valuable strategy for a self-employed individual is to hire your spouse and pay for his or her insurance through an HRA. We'll discuss this option in greater detail later in the book, but for now remember it as something you can bring up with your tax coach. It will allow you to use more pre-tax dollars on health insurance and save your partner from the trouble of finding and paying for a separate insurance policy.

For Businesses

As we discussed earlier, business owners face different insurance requirements depending on the size of the business. For companies with fewer than 50 full-time employees, you do not need to worry about the ACA unless you want to. If you are considering offering benefits, you can use the calculator at HealthCoverageGuide.org to determine the amount of your tax subsidy and get an idea of whether the government assistance will make offering insurance more affordable: http://healthcoverageguide.org/helpful-tools/small-business-health-insurance-premium-tax-credit-calculator/.

If you have more than 50 employees, you'll want to check the cost of coverage and determine whether offering insurance would be more affordable than paying the fee. If you have close to 50 employees, it may make more sense to pay the $2,000 fee for two or three people than to buy insurance for everyone. You can check the SHOP Marketplace at the small-business insurance exchange to review plans for your employees: https://www.healthcare.gov/small-businesses/provide-shop-coverage/.

A larger company may be able to avoid the ACA altogether by self-insuring its employees. One of the best options for this is a Medical Expense Reimbursement Program, or MERP. This allows you to reimburse the actual healthcare expenses paid by your workers. A MERP can be used to reimburse your employees for the cost of private health insurance premiums. Since individual insurance plans are currently cheaper than group policies, this allows both you and the employee to save money, and your expenses will be entirely tax deductible.

Thanks to the Affordable Care Act, Things Are Changing for the Better

There are three basic measures:

- Access
- Affordability
- Quality

When Affordable Care Act started, there were 50 plans. So far, there has been a 25% increase in issuers selling insurance in the marketplace starting in 2015. 7.3 million people signed up for marketplace plans, paid premiums, and have access to the ACA. In just one year, there was a 26% reduction in the number of uninsured adults. This means that, since 2013, 10.3 million adults are no longer uninsured. This is the key measure we should look at it because it is historic progress for something that has eluded our country for over a century. Getting better coverage and saving money are the key.

More than 8 million seniors are saving 11.5 billion dollars on prescriptions because the "donut hole"—which previously left seniors paying full price for prescriptions once a yearly maximum was reached— has been eliminated. Families do not have to worry about losing their homes or have their hard-earned savings wiped away by an accident or unexpected health diagnosis. There is security: if you lose your job, you can purchase marketplace coverage, even if you have a preexisting condition. And you won't lose your insurance or get cut off just because you get sick.

Since President Obama signed the ACA, there is evidence that we have bent the cost curve when it comes to healthcare. Healthcare inflation is at the lowest level in 50 years. If you're an employer, this means it is easier for you to hire workers. If you are an employee, it means you could be keeping more of your paycheck. And if you are a taxpayer, it means a healthier economy. Taken together, the evidence points to a clear conclusion: the ACA is working.

More Help

We have uncovered plenty of clues about the ACA and how it affects your taxes, but this is just scratching the surface of this complicated law. Since there is still so much confusion and misinformation out there about Obamacare, we decided to write a book dedicated to the topic. If you are interested in learning more, pick up a copy of *The Pocket Guide to Obamacare*.

As always, be sure to talk to your own private tax detective to be sure you are keeping up with changes to the law. Your Certified Tax Coach can help you make a personalized tax plan that will reduce your expenses while allowing you to enjoy the benefits of affordable health insurance.

ABOUT THE AUTHOR

Clinton Robinson, CTC

I am a Tax Preparer, Insurance Agent, and Community Activist, and I always attempt to pay it forward.

As a tax preparer for forty years, I found I would best serve the community on my own, studying the tax laws and rules for the best solution to the questions you have.

As a Certified Financial Planner and student at Yeshiva University, I was encouraged to become an insurance agent, estate planner, small-business trainer, and a Certified Tax Coach. I now represent my clients with the IRS, and I am studying to become an Enrolled Agent for the IRS.

As a former Councilman from the Third Ward of East Orange, NJ, I held the position of District Representative of NJ, NY, and PA. I am also a member of National Black Caucus Local Elected Officials (NBCLEO) and past president of the Rotary Club and Lions Club.

And as an author, I am writing more on the Affordable Care Act, and how it affects you from the lay person's— and not a political— point of view.

CR Pro Tax is located in East Orange, NJ, and we are also the proud owners of a Farmers Insurance Agency, providing automobile insurance to the general public.

"It's not how many can I get to help me, but rather how many can I help with the services provided by me."

I can be reached at (973) 675-2515 or clinton@crprotax.com, and you may visit my website at www.crprotax.com. You may also find more information in my other book "OBAMACARE and THE IRS UNCOVERED: What you MUST Know About the Affordable Care Act BEFORE Filing Your Tax Return."

Caught Unaware

Smart Tax Strategies for Healthcare Costs

By Kazim Qasim, EA, CTC

I n the previous chapter, we investigated the link between healthcare and taxes. The issue goes deeper than just the Affordable
Care Act, though, and understanding this relationship can help
you solve the mystery of how a smart tax strategy can cut down
the costs of your healthcare expenses.

For many people, healthcare costs are a major annual investment. If
you've been caught unaware by a serious illness or accident, the emergency medical costs can be devastating. Even if you're in good health,
the expenses of insurance and basic healthcare can add up quickly.
Healthcare costs have risen steadily over the past several years and will
probably continue to increase, meaning that a proactive strategy is im-
perative when it comes to minimizing the financial damage healthcare
costs can cause.

Fortunately, we can uncover a few clues that will help solve this
case. By combining this knowledge with a smart tax strategy, you can
keep your healthcare costs down without sacrificing the quality of your
care.

Smart Tax Strategies for Healthcare Costs

Any good tax detective will tell you that the key to good financial planning is learning to shift money that you are already spending from post-tax to pre-tax dollars. Since healthcare spending is an essential expense, spending it tax-free is the best way to reduce the overall financial impact. By using tax-free dollars to pay for your medical expenses, you can reduce your overall level of taxable income, which in turn will lower your total tax bill.

In order to shift your healthcare costs to tax-free dollars, you will need either a tax credit or a deduction. Let's investigate some ways that you can deduct medical expenses from your tax bill.

Tax Credits and Deductions

The first place to look for clues about a healthcare tax strategy is your available tax deductions. If your healthcare costs amount to more than 10% of your adjusted gross income, you can claim them as a deduction on your taxes. If you or your spouse is 65 or older, then you are allowed to use the lower 7.5% threshold until 2016.

This means that when you have high medical expenses in a given year, you can shift those costs into pre-tax dollars by deducting them from your taxes. You probably won't be able to claim a medical expense deduction every year, but it will come in handy during years when you have high costs due to surgeries, emergency-room visits, or other costly expenses.

Knowing that the deduction works this way, you can also make some smart choices about your medical care itself. For example, if you have already spent close to the 10%-figure in a given year for emergency medical costs, it might be a good idea to go ahead and opt for that elective procedure you have been putting off. If that procedure would put your medical costs over the 10% threshold, you will be able to spend pre-tax dollars on the procedure and effectively reduce its overall cost to you.

Other Deductible Expenses

Aside from the obvious itemized medical expense deduction, you can find a few other tax-saving opportunities if you dig a little deeper. Two of the most useful to know about are HSAs, which we will talk about in more detail a little bit later, and the tax credits offered through the ACA.

In our previous chapter, we discovered how people with incomes below 400% of the poverty line can receive tax credits to help offset the cost of insurance. What makes these tax credits unique is that they are applied directly to your insurance premiums rather than being figured into your taxes. This keeps more of your money in your pocket throughout the year. By combining this tax credit with the right kind of policy, you can uncover powerful savings.

What type of policy maximizes the benefits of the ACA tax credit? Let's investigate further.

Using a Health Savings Account

A Health Savings Account, or HSA, is a powerful multi-purpose tool for financial planning. Essentially, an HSA allows you to put money aside pre-tax for use for future medical expenses. What makes the HSA so valuable is that funds in it accrue and grow tax-free over time. Unused funds roll over from one year to the next. This means that the HSA doubles as an investment vehicle that can ultimately be cashed out for retirement.

To establish an HSA, you will need a high-deductible insurance policy. Right now, this means an individual deductible of $1,250 or family deductible of $2,500. This requirement can change, so be sure to stay abreast of these changes when it comes time to renew your policy, so that you can continue using your HSA. If you are buying insurance from the marketplace, look at bronze- and silver-level plans; these will most often have deductibles that match the HSA requirements.

Once you have purchased the appropriate insurance plan, you can set up the HSA through any bank of your choice. You can pay up to $3,300 per year into the account as an individual or $6,550 for a family plan. The money does roll over from one year to the next, allowing it to grow in value. This is especially helpful because just a few years of regular payments into the HSA can give you a safety net that will cover your out-of-pocket healthcare expenses. Since the out-of-pocket maximum for a bronze-level insurance plan is $6,267, a combination of insurance and an HSA could create full coverage within just two years of regular HSA contributions.

If you receive insurance through your employer, an HSA may have already been established for you as part of your benefits; check with your employer to see whether this is true in your case, or if you can add an HSA to your existing employer-provided insurance plan.

What Does an HSA Cover?

The money in your Health Savings Account can be used to pay for medical expenses outside of the cost of insurance premiums. This means that your HSA can be used for out-of-pocket costs like co-pays, coinsurance, and deductibles. It also means that you can use your HSA to pay for prescription drugs, whether or not prescriptions are covered by your insurance.

In the past, an HSA could also be used to pay for over-the-counter drugs, but this has been changed by the ACA. Now, you can only use money in an HSA for an over-the-counter medication if it is prescribed by a doctor.

Your HSA works like any other savings account in terms of gaining interest. You can access the funds with a debit card linked to the account. You can also withdraw the money as cash or even cash out the account, but you will suffer a 20% penalty if you withdraw funds before you turn 65. You're much better off letting money grow in the HSA, using the debit card for your medical expenses, and waiting until retirement to liquidate the account.

Is It Better to Use an HSA or a Lower Deductible Insurance Plan?

While HSAs can be very powerful, they are not the right tool for everyone. Depending on your situation, you might be better off paying higher premiums for a low-deductible insurance plan. For example, if you know that you will have high healthcare costs due to an ongoing medical condition, you might get more value from the low-deductible insurance plan since the out-of-pocket costs for your condition may exceed what you could otherwise comfortably deposit in an HSA.

If you are generally healthy, an HSA is a smart choice because it lets you accrue value from one year to the next, rather than sacrificing money toward premiums for years that you don't actually use your insurance. You can always use the HSA now and swap to a different insurance plan later in life when your needs change.

To determine which insurance strategy makes the most sense for you, you will need to do a cost analysis for both types of plans. Take into account your regular medical expenses and current income. If you qualify for a tax subsidy through the ACA, factor that into your decision as well. Your financial advisor can help guide you toward the right choice if you're still not sure which option is best for you.

Medical Expense Reimbursement Plans

While an HSA can be a very powerful tool, it is not your only option for paying medical expenses with pre-tax dollars. One of the most effective tax-planning strategies available is one that few people have heard about: the MERP, or Medical Expense Reimbursement Plan.

A MERP is an alternative to regular group health insurance for employees. Rather than purchasing insurance, an employer can use the plan to reimburse the actual medical expenses of workers. The money in the MERP can go toward reimbursing out-of-pocket expenses as well as the insurance premiums themselves. This is a mutually beneficial situation for workers and employees as it allows the employee to buy whatever insurance policy he wishes while still receiving financial assistance from work.

In some situations, a MERP can also be used to pay for your own medical expenses. This is trickier to pull off, but let's piece together the clues to see how it all comes together.

What Does a MERP Cover?

MERPs are very flexible and can be used to cover any necessary medical expenses:

- Health insurance premiums.
- Prescription drugs.
- Insurance co-pays, deductibles, and other out-of-pocket expenses.
- Dental, vision, and other medical costs that may be uninsured.
- Medical equipment, including things like wheelchairs or medically required whirlpools.
- Specialty therapies.

As its name suggests, a MERP works on a reimbursement basis. The employee would pay for the expense out-of-pocket and be reimbursed by the employer from the money set aside to cover the MERP. The employer would then be able to deduct that expense from the company's taxes as an itemized deduction.

Using a MERP As a Business Owner

Businesses of any size can establish a MERP. There are just a few rules to keep in mind when setting one up:

- The plan must cover all full-time employees over the age of 25.
- The same level of benefits must be offered to all employees, although, of course, individual reimbursement amounts will vary between workers from one year to the next.
- If your business is affiliated with another business and gains more than 50% of its profits from that business, both will be treated as one business as far as the MERP is concerned. In

other words, you can't set up a MERP for the employees in one half of your business while ignoring the other half.

The scope of a MERP means that it works best for smaller companies. If you run a larger business, you might be better off self-insuring your workers through a captive insurance company or a standard group plan. For small businesses, however, a MERP will minimize your out-of-pocket expenses and allow you to deduct 100% of the cost.

In order to set up a MERP for your workers, you will need to draft a detailed plan explaining the value of the benefits, and what exactly you will cover. Work with your financial advisor to set this up and ensure that everything is in order. If everything is explained clearly in the beginning, it will save you from trouble down the line.

Business Designations and MERPs

The rules for using a MERP will vary slightly between business types. If you know in advance that you might want to set up a MERP, you can establish your business as the most tax-advantageous designation:

- Sole proprietors cannot use a MERP for themselves, but they can establish one for any employees they may hire, including family members.

- The primary partners in a partnership cannot have a MERP, but one can be set up for a silent partner who owns no interest in the company, as well as for any employees.

- C corporations are the most versatile; even the owner can establish a MERP for him- or herself.

- In an S corporation, anyone with less than 2% ownership in the company can have a MERP.

As you can see, most business designations will not allow you to set up a MERP for yourself as the business owner. However, you can work around this by hiring your spouse. Let's investigate that option further.

Hiring Your Spouse

The greatest strength of a medical reimbursement account is that it can be used to shift your own medical expenses to tax-free money. This works because a MERP extends benefits to an entire family. Therefore, if you set up a MERP for your spouse, you can use it to reimburse the whole household's medical expenses.

To set this up, you will need to hire your spouse as a bona fide employee of the company. Your spouse's work contributions will need to be in line with the amount of benefits given. In other words, a few hours of work per year would not be enough to justify a MERP, but ongoing and necessary work for your business would be allowable.

It is likely that your spouse may already be doing important tasks to help with your business, such as keeping your books, answering the phone, or fielding business emails. Since you can pay in benefits, you don't need to set up a payroll or W-2 for your spouse. You will, however, need to document what work your spouse is doing and have a thorough plan document in place for the MERP. Keeping track of how many hours your spouse works, and what is done during that time, will protect you if you are audited, and prove that the MERP is appropriate compensation.

Putting It All Together

If there is one thing that you will learn quickly as a detective, it is that no single piece of evidence can solve a whole case. It is the same with being a tax detective: no single tax-saving tip will work as well as when all of the pieces are put together into a cohesive strategy.

In the case of medical expenses, you can maximize the effectiveness of the tips we have uncovered throughout this chapter by combining them:

- First, hire your spouse as an employee and set up a MERP for both of you, taking advantage of the fact that a MERP will pay for a household's medical expenses.

- Next, have your spouse purchase a high-deductible family in-surance policy from the health insurance exchange, and be sure you are covered by it.

- If applicable, use your ACA tax credit to reduce the amount of your monthly premiums.

- Obtain an HSA that is compatible with your spouse's insurance, and deposit as much into it each year as you can afford.

- Use the HSA to pay for things like prescription drugs and out-of-pocket co-pays. When you reimburse the HSA, deduct that reimbursement using the MERP.

Doing this, you will be able to deduct the cost of your insurance premiums from your taxes, since they will be a reimbursable expense through the MERP. You will also be able to grow value in your HSA from one year to the next, ultimately putting it toward an emergency nest egg or even retirement down the line. Between the money in your HSA and the tax-deductible quality of any reimbursed medical pro-cedures, your overall out-of-pocket healthcare expenses will be mini-mized.

Of course, this strategy will not work in every situation, and not every household will be able to put it into action. However, nearly ev-eryone can take advantage of at least some of the tips in this chapter, and those can be combined with other strategies to save money on different expenses later down the line. You can discuss your options with a tax professional to be sure you are maximizing your savings opportunities.

Let us use the example of James who is a real-estate broker and has a small maintenance business set up as an LLC. His annual health insurance premiums are $6,000, and he has out-of-pocket medical ex-penses of $5,500. He is in the process of implementing a combination of the tips covered in this chapter. After full implementation, James can expect to reduce his annual tax expense by more than $3,300. By combining some of these tips, James is maximizing his tax savings, and you can too.

ABOUT THE AUTHOR

Kazim Qasim, EA, CTC

Kazim Qasim has been involved in accounting since 1978, being employed in the private sector across many industries. He graduated from Lehman's College of the City University of New York, receiving The New York State Society of Certified Public Accountants award as the top accounting graduate. As an Enrolled Agent, Kazim has the ability to represent clients across the country before any branch of the IRS. But the real value of his expertise lies in the Certified Tax Coach designation, whereby he delights clients by freeing up unknown avenues of cash flow for expansion, renovation, new equipment, or any other business and personal needs.

Kazim performs a diagnosis of tax returns to uncover "business tax obesity" or any of its symptoms.

Then, he dons his detective hat, seeking clues within the tax codes to defend against this monster disease. A treatment plan is then formulated by utilizing customized prescriptions of available credits, deductions, and loopholes to cure this debilitating illness and any related symptoms. Although it was not known as proactive tax planning at the time, his first instance utilizing these strategies was in 2004, when, as the new CFO of a New York City business, he was able to reduce the tax expense by more than $100,000 in the first year.

Kazim can be reached at (407) 583-6444 or email him at kazim@azsaccounting.com.

www.azsaccounting.com

CHAPTER 7

Into Thin Air

Creating Income with Less Tax

By Robert Henderson Jr., CFP®, CTC

T hroughout this book, we have solved many mysteries about financial planning. Many of the clues we have seen have led to the same conclusion: you can save a lot of money on taxes by simply shifting your expenses into deductible categories. This allows you to reduce your overall tax burden while saving money on expenses you would be paying anyway, and it's a smart tax strategy for business owners in particular as the available deductions are so valuable.

Tax planning is not limited to this strategy, however. A clever tax detective knows that there is another powerful method for minimizing your taxes: growing your wealth through tax-free income. This is the cornerstone of retirement planning, and it builds upon some of the principles we investigated in earlier chapters.

Let's look at some clues for how you can create tax-free income with a smart investment strategy.

Four Types of Investment Accounts

The point of retirement planning is to secure a healthy financial future by setting aside money to use after you've left the workforce. For most people, retirement planning is also a method for growing wealth in order to establish a family legacy: the money that's not spent during your retirement passes forward to your heirs, who in turn can grow that wealth through additional investments.

It is certainly possible to save for retirement simply by socking money away in a drawer, but that is not a very efficient system. Successful retirement planning requires an investment. When you invest, your money grows in value, allowing you to reach much greater wealth than you could otherwise.

With that in mind, the first clue that you discover when exploring retirement plans is that not all investments are created equally. Some types of investment accounts will yield much greater rewards than others when it comes to tax planning. Understanding your options allows you to choose the best strategy for your financial plans.

In general, there are four main ways that the money you invest can be taxed, and the type of investment account you use determines the taxes you pay. Let's investigate these to see whether we can find a few clues about which investments are the most tax-friendly.

Taxable All the Time

Some investments offer very few tax benefits. You must pay tax on the money in these accounts every year, not just when the money is withdrawn for use. Depending on the type of investment, you may be taxed for capital gains rather than income, but you will still face a tax bill. Many common investments are taxed this way:

- Bank CDs
- Savings accounts
- Mutual funds
- Stock-trading accounts

Many of these investments are more commonly used for income than retirement planning due to their tax structure. They are not necessarily designed well for long-term investments since you will be stuck paying taxes on their gains. While such investments do have their place, they are not very tax-efficient. When it comes to setting money aside for retirement, there are much better options.

Tax-Deferred

Some investment vehicles allow you to invest and grow wealth without incurring any taxes. Taxes are due when you withdraw money from these accounts. Two common examples are annuities and non-deductible, traditional IRAs.

A tax-deferred investment can become an integral part of a smart tax strategy, but it can also be problematic, as you never know for sure what the future may hold. If you withdraw money at a time when your income is low, you won't need to pay much in taxes. If, however, you must withdraw money while your income from other sources is high, you can lose a substantial amount of your investment.

One helpful thing to remember about tax-deferred accounts is that you will only be taxed on the gains, not your basis. In other words, the money that you initially paid into the account will not be subject to any additional taxes. This makes these accounts useful in some contexts, but they should never be your first choice when looking to set aside money for long-term growth.

Deductible Contributions

These investment wrappers allow you to place pre-tax dollars into an investment that then grows in a tax-deferred environment until you are ready to withdraw the funds. We have touched on these investments in the past as they are very popular retirement planning options. Here are a few of the most common plans utilizing deductible contributions:

- Traditional IRAs
- 401(k)s
- SEPs

You may notice that these plans are common vehicles for employer-sponsored retirement accounts. This is because the tax-deductible nature of contributions makes them very attractive to businesses look-ing to trim costs. From the perspective of an individual, however, these accounts can leave something to be desired.

As we discovered earlier, tax-deferred accounts can be a gamble. If you can put off your withdrawals until you have reached a lower tax bracket, you can enjoy some tax savings. However, if your investments do well, you will still lose a large chunk of your wealth to taxes.

You face another problem with traditional IRAs: if you pass away before exhausting the funds within the IRA, your heirs will be taxed both income tax and inheritance tax on the money inside. This makes a traditional IRA a terrible vehicle for estate planning.

You can avoid these issues by moving some of your most valuable tax-deferred assets into a tax-exempt wrapper. Let's investigate that op-tion now.

Tax-Exempt

A tax-exempt investment is one that uses after-tax contributions as the basis for the investment. You get no deductions for putting money in, but once invested, you will never be charged for the interest these investments earn. When you withdraw funds, you will not have to pay any taxes. This concept is often referred to as "paying taxes on the seed rather than on the harvest." For example, imagine you wake up one day, and you are a farmer. The tax collector gives you two options for paying taxes: (a) pay tax on the seed or (b) pay tax on your crop (har-vest) after it has grown and become plentiful. Which option do you choose? By paying taxes on the seed now, you are paying taxes on a smaller amount because the seeds have not produced a harvest yet. When the harvest comes, no taxes are due.

The best-known tax-exempt investment is the Roth IRA. Another option, which you may not have considered, is investment-grade life insurance. We will look at insurance in greater depth shortly. For now, let's focus on the Roth IRA.

Like a traditional IRA, a Roth IRA is the vehicle for cash investments. The actual nature of the investments is up to you: you can use the funds in an IRA to buy stocks, bonds, even real estate. Since Roth IRAs are so powerful, they have a yearly contribution cap of $5,500 if you are under age 50, or $6,500 if you are age 50 or older, according to 2015 contribution rules. You can only utilize a ROTH IRA if your income is below $122,000 for an individual or $188,000 for a married couple filing jointly.

Just How Powerful Is a Roth IRA?

To get an idea of just how valuable the tax-free wealth generation of a Roth IRA can be, let's look at a couple of examples. One real-life success story concerns Max R. Levchin, the founder of Yelp. Before his company grew to its current size, he filled a Roth IRA with shares. Now, that those shares are worth more, the value of the IRA has grown to an astonishing $95 million, and he won't need to pay a cent in taxes as long as he waits until he turns 59 and a half before withdrawing the money and has satisfied the 5-year contribution period. Moreover, any money he leaves in that Roth IRA will pass to his children tax-free after his death.

Of course, most of us don't have ownership of a massive company with such valuable shares, but we can still benefit from the tax-free growth of wealth accumulated in a Roth IRA. Look at it this way: if you started with just $1 in an investment that doubled each year over a 20-year period, you would end up with $1,048,076. If that same investment were taxed every year as regular income, you would walk away with just $127,482 after 20 years!

Roll Over Your Assets

Seeing the power of a Roth IRA in action brings us to the next mystery: how can you incorporate a Roth IRA into your current financial plan? After all, many people already have retirement accounts set up through their employers, and as we have seen, those accounts are not always the most tax-advantageous options. Fortunately, there is a simple solution: you can roll funds from your current investment accounts into a Roth IRA.

For example, imagine that you already have a 401(k) or traditional IRA. You funded that account with tax-deductible money and are not currently paying taxes on the gains. If you roll those funds into a Roth IRA, you will need to pay some taxes now, but all future gains will be tax-free. If you have an investment that is doing well and looks like it might grow in value, moving it to a Roth IRA is one of the smartest things you can do for your long-term financial well-being.

Knowing when to roll funds into a Roth IRA takes some market shrewdness, so it is a good idea to attempt this only if you have the backing of an experienced financial professional who can help you decide which of your investments are most likely to become profitable, so that you can maximize the effectiveness of this strategy.

Unexpected Retirement-Planning Options

We have already investigated several well-known retirement investments in this chapter and others throughout this book. These are just a few of the options available to you. There are some lesser-known investments that offer significant benefits and can play a major role in your tax strategy. Let's delve into this mystery to uncover a few clues about these little-known opportunities.

Solo 401(k)

If you work for an employer, it is likely that you have a 401(k) option available to you. If you are self-employed, however, you can create a 401(k) for yourself. In fact, a Solo 401(k) can be an especially powerful financial planning tool because it is not subject to the same limitations as a standard 401(k).

A Solo 401(k) allows you to set aside up to $17,500 per year to invest. This is much more attractive than the $5,500 limit of a traditional IRA. More importantly, the funds you place in a solo 401(k) can be invested in any vehicle you like; you can even lend money out and charge interest like a lending institution. The Solo 401(K) is a powerful financial planning tool for small-business owners with no employees and for husband-and-wife teams. You have the choice of making the funds deductible and tax-deferred, or tax-free like a Roth IRA.

If you hire your children, you can even use the Solo 401(k) as a vehicle for establishing a college fund. In a small business that employs only you and your spouse or children, you can set up a Solo 401(k) for your employees. By paying your children's wages into a Roth 401(k), you set them up to receive the full benefits of tax-free income down the line.

The other great benefit of a Solo 401(k) is that it is self-guided. When you take a traditional 401(k), your investment options are limited by your employer. But with the Solo 401(K), you are the boss, you are the HR department. When you establish your own plan, you are free to make investments that suit your particular needs: stocks, bonds, mutual funds, real estate, precious metals, and businesses are just a few of the available options.

Life Insurance

We touched on life insurance as one of the tax-free investment opportunities available to people planning their retirement earlier. For most people, life insurance is simply a way to cover end-of-life expenses or provide financial assistance to their surviving loved ones. However, certain types of life insurance plans can become powerful investments in their own right.

To benefit, you will need a permanent type of life insurance, such as whole of universal life. These plans are more expensive than basic term life insurance, but they last indefinitely as long as you continue making payments. Some plans offer payment options that enable you to make premium payments for only 10, 15, 20, or 25 years when the policy is paid up. You can also help increase your cash value by over-funding the policy, which basically means paying over and above the base premium amount. Each time you pay your life insurance premiums, a portion of the money is invested. The policy then builds cash value over time. This value is added to the death benefit built into the policy, and it can be accessed while the policyholder is still alive.

The rate of return for life insurance investments is usually pretty good. You can generally expect to earn about 4% to 6% on your investments once the associated fees have been covered. More importantly, the cash value of your life insurance is not taxed. Since you pay premiums with after-tax dollars, the money in the life insurance plan grows tax-free just as it would with a Roth IRA. We can call this a Super Roth IRA.

Investment-grade life insurance has some benefits over Roth IRAs. For one, there are no contribution limitations—you can place as much money into your insurance as you wish. Additionally, you can contribute to a whole or universal life insurance plan regardless of your income, allowing high-earners to sidestep barriers placed on Roth IRAs.

Annuities

When shopping for life insurance, you may notice that most insurance companies also sell annuities. An annuity is another valuable retirement planning tool because it fills in the gaps of other investments. In general, an annuity is meant to provide supplemental income when a retiree has exhausted his other resources.

You pay into an annuity much as you would a pension plan. You can obtain this either by paying installments throughout your working life or by making a single payment today. Either way, when you obtain the annuity, it comes with a promise and a contract that you will receive a predefined payout in the future at regular intervals. This future income is calculated based on your life expectancy and the amount of money you have invested into the annuity. In other words, a 50-year-old who invests $100,000 in an annuity will generally receive a lower monthly payout benefit amount than a 60-year-old. This is because the longer you are expected to live, the less money you will receive per installment.

The money you receive is made up in part of your initial basis as well as an additional amount. Only the additional amount is taxed; the rest is returned to you tax-free. Annuities provide several attractive benefits:

- There are no annual contribution limits for annuities like there are for IRAs.
- The funds are invested and grow tax-deferred.
- Annuities provide a guaranteed retirement income depending on the type of annuity.
- The money in your annuity will pass directly to your beneficiaries without probate when you die.
- Your beneficiaries will receive a guaranteed minimum death benefit regardless of the market activity of your investments, if elected in the contract.

As you can see, an annuity can make a powerful addition to your investment portfolio, and therefore it is an excellent part of any retirement plan.

Social Security Strategies

When planning for retirement, it is smart to consider how your various investment accounts will interact with your Social Security income. Although Social Security payments themselves are generally not subject to taxes, the income you earn can affect the amount of tax you pay on other investments. Additionally, your income can affect the amount of Social Security that you receive. Since you have paid into Social Security throughout your working life, it is worth the effort to squeeze every penny of value from your Social Security payments.

The most important thing you can do to maximize the value of your Social Security is to wait as long as possible before using it. Taking out Social Security early minimizes the value of payments for the rest of your life, so delaying it is always the best strategy. This is especially true if you have income from other sources. Between the ages of 62 and 65, income above $15,120 will reduce your Social Security by $1 for every $2 over that threshold. Once you turn 65, your income threshold rises to $40,800, and you lose just $1 per $3 earned.

With those figures in mind, your best bet is to live off the money in your IRAs or other investment accounts for the first few years of retirement. Once you no longer have money coming in from cashed-out retirement accounts, you will be safe to start taking Social Security payments. Also, bear in mind that since Roth IRAs and other tax-free investments are not taxed as income, they will not affect your Social Security. Feel free to structure your withdrawals, so that your Roth accounts coincide with Social Security payments.

Let's Review Our Clues:

- You can save money on your taxes by creating tax-free sources of income.

- Different types of investments are taxed in different ways, and understanding these is the key to developing a smart retirement strategy.

- Investments to consider for tax reduction are those that grow tax-free and are not taxed on payout. These include Roth IRAs and investment-grade life insurance.

- A Solo 401(k) offers more flexibility than an employer-sponsored plan, and it is a valuable tool for sole proprietors and self-employed small-business owners with few or no employees.

- An annuity helps to provide supplemental retirement income to fill in the gaps of your other investments.

- Life insurance can be a powerful investment tool thanks to its favorable growth and tax-free payout, especially when you overfund it.

- Understanding how Social Security payments interact with your other forms of retirement income will help you obtain maximum benefits from your tax strategy.

Securities offered through IFS Securities, Inc. Member FINRA/SPIC, 3414 Peachtree Road NE, Suite 1020 Atlanta, GA 30326
IFS Securities and The Henderson Financial Group Inc. are not affiliated

ABOUT THE AUTHOR

Robert Henderson Jr., CFP®, CTC

I am Robert Henderson Jr., Certified Financial Planner and Certified Tax Coach. In addition to these designations, I hold Series 7 and 63 Securities Licenses; Life, Health & Annuity License; and a Real Estate Broker License. I am a member of the Financial Planning Association, Certified Financial Planning Association, and The Miami Board of Realtors.

With all of these tools, I use my knowledge and expertise to make financial planning child's play for my clients. By using analogies and metaphors, I teach people how to understand the seemingly complex world of financial planning and tax reduction, and break down concepts to a level that anyone can understand. I show people how to take charge of their financial *house,* so that their financial future starts to feel more like a *home.*

For the past twenty-five years, I have successfully headed The Henderson Financial Group, a full-service financial planning firm with offices in South Florida and Atlanta. The vast majority of my clients are business owners and pre-retirees. While people usually come to me for my expertise and guidance in establishing a financial plan, what they walk away with is actually a sense of relief, a feeling of confidence, and a deep understanding about the direction and necessary steps to secure their financial future.

I facilitate my appointments with clients similar to a physician. During our initial consultation, I get to know the client and their background (financial habits) before reviewing, diagnosing, and ultimately prescribing a financial plan. When people know their finances are in order, it is better for everyone. They say money isn't everything, but it is right up there next to air—it is needed to survive. Money gives you more options!

When I am not educating my clients and demystifying the world of investing, finances and taxes, I enjoy reading, running marathons, traveling across the world, playing piano, learning Spanish as a second language, and giving back to my community. For the past seven years, I have served as a Guardian Ad Litem for disadvantaged and underprivileged children of Broward County, Florida. Every Saturday morning at 8 am, you can hear me talk finance and taxes live on 880thebiz.com. The show is down-to-earth and easy to understand. It is aired from a beautiful studio in Miami, FL, so if you are in Miami Dade or surrounding counties, you can tune in to 880AM on your radio dial.

You can reach me at (305) 825-1444 or email me at Robert.Henderson@ifssecurities.com.

The Henderson Financial Group
5783A NW 151st Street
Miami Lakes, FL 33014

Tel. (305) 825-1444

Email: Robert.Henderson@ifssecurities.com

CHAPTER 8

The Legend of Real-Estate Tax Strategies

By Ronald A. Mermer, CPA, CGMA, CTC, CCPS

W hat is arguably the biggest mystery faced by anyone looking to live a better life? It is the mystery of why some people work hard throughout their lives without ever getting ahead while others are able to accrue massive wealth with seemingly little effort.

There are a lot of variables that go into this, so solving this mystery isn't an easy feat. However, there is one major clue you can uncover that will point you in the right direction: the wealthiest people nearly always gain their wealth through investments. This makes sense when you consider the difference between investments and active income.

Investments are mostly passive. Once you set them up, they generally take care of themselves, giving you more time and freedom to tend to other things. Your time is valuable, and investments take up less time than active labor does. This allows you to make many investments throughout your life, and the returns on those investments can add up quickly to create a powerful income-generating machine.

We touched on investments in our retirement planning chapter, but now let's focus on one especially valuable type of investment: real estate.

Why Real Estate Is a Smart Investment

Real-estate investing is one of the oldest traditions in America. The founding fathers themselves were landowners who used their land to build wealth and establish a financial legacy for their heirs, and today's real-estate investors are no different.

Real estate is an especially valuable investment because it creates profits in two ways. First, a piece of real estate will appreciate over time, especially if it is located in a nice neighborhood where property values rise. Second, an investment property can bring in monthly income when you rent it out to a tenant. This allows you to create both short- and long-term profits from your investment property, something that is not possible with many other types of investments.

The basic premise behind real-estate investing is simple: you start by buying a property, preferably the most affordable property in the best neighborhood. Next, you rent out the property and use that income to cover the overhead costs of owning and maintaining it. A portion of the rental income should go into your pocket each month. After a few years, when the property has increased in value, you can sell it and pocket the profits.

Now is a particularly good time to get involved in real estate as there is little competition. Many people mistakenly believe that real-estate investing is no longer profitable, so home prices are remaining low. Property continues to appreciate, however, so your long-term investment will remain secure. Additionally, young people are waiting longer to buy their first houses, and they are much more likely to rent their homes than previous generations were. This means that there is a constant demand for rental properties, which will help you to secure short-term income while you wait for your investment to come to fruition.

Investing vs. Flipping

The process described above is not the same as "flipping" a house for money. Flipping involves buying a low-priced home, often one that requires significant repairs, and putting the work into it to boost its value before selling it. House flipping usually involves selling a property quickly, and while it can be lucrative, it is not an investment. It is also not a sound strategy for many people, as it requires a lot of hard work and knowledge to rehabilitate a home while keeping costs low.

The biggest problem with the "fix and flip" approach is that you miss many valuable tax benefits. If you are selling more than a couple properties per year, the IRS will classify you as a property dealer rather than an investor. This will shift all of your profits out of capital gains and into pure income, and you will be taxed as a business. While there are some tax benefits to owning a business, property dealing is not the most tax-effective choice. It is much safer and more tax-preferred to buy houses at a slower rate and allow them to accrue value over time.

Using Leverage

While it may seem counterintuitive, the key to a successful real-estate investment lies in financing the homes that you buy. In real estate, the use of a mortgage to finance your investment is called leverage because it can give you quite a bit more profit-generating power than you would otherwise have.

Look at it this way: Imagine that you have $500,000 ready to invest in a property. You buy a home outright for that amount and charge $3,200 per month for rent. You need to pay out $525 per month in property taxes and insurance, so you have a net income of $2,675 per month.

Now, imagine that instead of buying one property, you used your $500,000 to put a down payment on five houses of the same value. Now you have invested $100,000 in each of five properties. You charge the same $3,200 rent per month for each home. You take out $2,551 for each home to cover your mortgage, insurance, and taxes, leaving you with a total income of $3,245 per month.

That extra money isn't worth much in its own right, but the value of this plan comes when it is time to sell the properties. Multiple properties represent a diversified investment, and every property you own has a chance to grow significantly in value. By diversifying, you are not taking a gamble on which property will gain the most value. You are taking fate into your own hands by spreading out your investment over a variety of neighborhoods and property types. Since the costs of the mortgage will be paid by your rental income, you have nothing to lose by using leverage, and you stand to gain quite a lot.

Maximize Your Investment With an IRA

We have already investigated how IRAs can be a very tax-advantageous method of setting aside retirement funds. As you may recall from our retirement chapter, an IRA can be used for nearly any type of investment, including real estate. This allows you to take full advantage of the tax benefits of an IRA while investing in rental properties.

To use an IRA for this purpose, you will need a self-directed IRA managed by a trustee. This trustee should be the one managing the funds for investments, and the transactions (rental income and expenses) will flow through him. Note that you cannot use the IRA for a home that you occupy: the purchase must be of a new home, and you cannot live in that property or use it as a vacation home. As with any other IRA investment, your profits will accrue tax-deferred or tax-free as the home gains value or is eventually sold.

Tax Strategies for Maximizing Real-Estate Investments

Now that we have looked at some of the clues about how real-estate investments can be so profitable, and why they are a smart choice for people looking to grow their wealth, let's delve deeper into the mystery of how you can get the most from your property investments by using a smart tax strategy.

Let's go back to the example we used earlier of the $500,000 homes that you are using leverage to finance. After a couple of years, one home's value may have risen up to $530,000, or by 6%. You don't owe any additional taxes on the home even though it is increased in value.

At this point, or later when the home has gained even more value, you can refinance the property and harvest some equity from it. Say you wait a couple more years and harvest $100,000 in equity from the property after refinancing. That $100,000 is tax-free and goes straight into your pocket.

If this ability to gain tax-free profits from a property investment were the only benefit of buying real estate, it would already be a great idea. However, there are even more tax strategies for squeezing extra value out of your rental property.

Deductions and Depreciation

We have talked about deductions before in the business chapter. As you recall, deductions are powerful because they allow you to reduce your overall taxable income by shifting purchases into pre-tax dollars. A new set of deductions applies specifically to property, creating ample new opportunities for tax savings.

When you own a piece of property, you are able to deduct depreciation on the home and its components. You can also make deductions on the cost of repairs that you make to the home as part of its regular upkeep. These deductions reduce your overhead as the investment grows in value.

To maximize your deductible expenses, it helps to classify the work you do on a home as a repair rather than an improvement. Improvements, which boost the base value of the home, are not tax deductible since they ultimately work toward increasing the property's value. Improvements do eventually depreciate, but you won't be able to claim that depreciation right away. A repair, however, is deductible immediately since it only returns the property to its original state.

When looking at a home, think in terms of repairs rather than improvements. For example, it might be advantageous to replace a few shingles rather than an entire roof, or you might want to replace the carpeting throughout a house rather than lay down linoleum. Whenever you do get work done on the property, be sure that you save receipts and get separate invoices for repairs and improvements if they are done at the same time. This will make it easier to itemize them later on.

Cost Segregation

Every part of your home is expected to depreciate, and some parts of it depreciate at a faster rate than others. Cost segregation is the act of identifying the separate parts of a home and claiming depreciation on them individually, making the most of their separate depreciation rates. Several parts of your property can be depreciated on their own schedules:

- The house itself.
- Any related structures on the property, like a shed or garage.
- Improvements to the land, including landscaping, walkways, and driveways.
- Components of the home, such as the roof, flooring, cabinets, tile, etc.
- Essential appliances and other parts of the home, like an air conditioner or water heater.

Since each category depreciates at a different rate, you will want to allocate your basis to the category with the shortest lifespan. For example, a home's components depreciate after five years. Therefore, it can make a lot more sense to put money into updating a property's cabinets and appliances than to put a lot of your basis into the roof, which takes much longer to depreciate.

Specialized Tax Credits

Most of the properties that you invest in will be residential homes rented out to individuals. If you have obtained a few types of specialty properties, however, you may qualify for some additional tax benefits.

For example, non-residential structures built before 1936 can qualify as historic buildings. The same is true for any property that has been certified as a historical site. If you buy a historical property, you can receive a tax credit of 10% to 20% toward the cost of rehabilitating the structure.

There are a few limitations to this, and it can be tricky to set up. If you are interested in this tax credit, it is a good idea to speak with your financial advisor, so he can help you work out the logistics for your specific situation.

Making a Business

If you want to make the most of your real-estate investments, you might want to consider turning your activities into an active business rather than a passive one. Doing so allows you to take advantage of the benefits we have discussed up to this point in addition to many of the tax perks associated with running a small business. Remember that your business is one of renting out the properties, not selling them; you are not trying to become a property dealer but rather a real-estate professional who sometimes sells investment properties.

Many things can be deducted throughout the course of your real-estate activities:

- Management expenses for renting out the property. This includes costs incurred while collecting profits or preparing the home for rental.
- Mortgage interest on your repairs, improvements, additions, and equipment.
- Travel expenses incurred while managing your properties, such as gas and lodging to travel to an investment property away from home.
- Meal and entertainment expenses incurred while meeting with clients, prospective renters, etc.
- Home office expenses for setting up a dedicated office space for the real-estate business.
- Wages and benefits for any employees you might hire, including family members.

- Insurance costs, including property insurance for the rentals and any benefits you may offer your employees.
- Professional services, including financial advice and legal counsel.

All of these deductions can be used to offset other income or simply reduce the amount you are spending on your real-estate activities. Let's investigate a few of the most valuable opportunities more closely:

- Consider hiring a family member to help with your property rental business. This allows you to maintain a passive income while enjoying the tax break from setting up employee benefits. You may even want to consider paying your employee in benefits-only rather than wages, so that you can skip the W-2s.
- If you hire your children, you can pay them up to $6,100 per person without incurring any taxes on those wages. You can put this money into an investment account on their behalf and establish a tax-preferred savings fund for college.
- When you make real estate an active business rather than a passive activity, you can claim your losses to offset gains from other sources of income. This way, you can claim up to $25,000 in real-estate rental loss allowance per year, which can make a serious impact on your other income. (Certain income limitations apply.)

As you can see, setting up an active real-estate business can be very tax-advantageous, especially when you combine these deductions with the deductions already inherent in property investing.

We have gone a long way toward solving the mystery of how you can use real estate to generate massive amounts of income, but many additional factors can come into play. Since investing can be complex, it is always a good idea to consult with a financial advisor before you jump into property investing. Your Certified Tax Coach will be able to walk you through your options and help you set up the investment plan that will work best for your particular situation, income, and goals.

Let's Review Our Clues:

- Working hard at a job isn't the best way to amass wealth. To really get the most value from your time, you need investment income.

- Real estate is one of the oldest and most stable investments, and it has some tax advantages that make it especially valuable.

- The idea behind property investing is to buy a home and rent it out, using the rental income to cover your overhead costs while you wait for the property to increase in value. The rental income will keep you from paying too much out of pocket, protecting your profit margins.

- Using a self-directed IRA to house your investment can be a very smart way to minimize taxes. By coupling the tax benefits of an IRA with those of real estate, you can see your investment grow in a tax-deferred setting.

- Use leverage to diversify your investments and obtain multiple properties, maximizing your chance of securing high profits when a property value increases.

- You can take multiple deductions for your investment property, including depreciation and repairs, to help offset income gains.

- Setting up your real-estate management activities as an active business allows you to take advantage of many other tax benefits, including the opportunity to hire family members and write off their benefits on your taxes.

- Operating as an LLC will provide asset protection as well as advantageous tax benefits. To provide the best protection, each property should be owned by a separate LLC.

- Owning multiple investment properties can be both profitable and tax advantageous. With proper documentation that meets the requirements of being a real-estate professional, you can have deductible losses in excess of the $25,000 annual allowance. One of my clients, who owned several rental properties, was never advised to maintain records to document that he qualified as a real-estate professional. I advised my client as to what was needed, and the deductible rental loss exceed $100,000, saving my client over $40,000 of additional taxes. With proper planning, real-estate investments save you money on taxes while you profit from your investments.

ABOUT THE AUTHOR

RONALD A. MERMER, CPA, CGMA, CTC, CCPS

Ronald A. Mermer is president of Ronald A. Mermer , CPA, P.C. located in the beautiful Hudson Valley Region of New York State. Ron has been practicing accounting and tax planning for over 30 years and strives to help his clients save money by legally reducing their tax liabilities through proactive tax planning. Ron's philosophy is to help clients keep more of what they work hard for.

In addition to co-authoring *The Tax Detective: Uncovering the Mystery of Tax Planning and Keeping More of What You Earn*, Ron is a best-selling author who has coauthored *Secrets of a Tax-Free Life*, *Surprising Write-Off Strategies Most Business Owners Miss*, *The Pocket Guide to Obamacare*, *57 Ways to Grow Your Business*, and *The Ten Most Expensive Tax Mistakes That Cost Real Estate Agents Thousands*. Ronald was selected for inclusion in the 2011 Hudson Valley Wealth Managers, which was recognized by *Hudson Valley Magazine* and has been added to The Registry of Business Excellence by the American Registry.

Ron is licensed as a Certified Public Accountant in NY, FL, and CT and is also a Chartered Global Management Accountant, a Certified Tax Coach, and a Certified College Planning Specialist.

Ron can be reached at (845) 897-5108 or at ron@mermcpas.com. View his website at www.proactivetaxplan.com or www.mermcpas.com

CHAPTER 9

The Case of the Mysterious Financial Advisor

 Tax Secrets They Forget to Tell You

By Lynn A. Schmidt, EA, CTC, CFS®, CSA, ARA

F or most of us, taxes are a mystery. Between the always-changing tax laws, the dense specialized vocabulary, and the exhausting strings of numbers, you might find yourself feeling out of your depth (or out of your mind) when it comes time to pay your taxes. At the same time, you know that your financial well-being is greatly affected by your tax bill. After all, taxes can be your single biggest expense, and it's a cost that only increases as you become more financially successful. When you have your taxes prepared at the end of the year, you hope that your tax preparer can advise you on how to reduce those costs in the future.

Fortunately for you, there are smart tax strategies that can be used to save money every year. In fact, many tax trimming techniques could actually go on to make you money by utilizing a variety of financial and tax strategies. The trick is simply knowing that those opportunities exist. They are often not common knowledge and, as a result, underuti-lized by the average taxpayer. Many tax preparers themselves are either unaware of valuable tax breaks or simply lack the creativity to applythem to their clients' finances. That's one reason you should always check the credentials of the tax preparer and be sure you are working with a professionally licensed and specially trained one.

If you think that you may not be receiving the best service or advice possible, it might be time to look for a different tax professional. After all, the reason you're paying someone to do your taxes for you is so that you can obtain the best results and pay the lowest tax legally possible.

What is a Tax Detective?

Like any mystery, those that lie within the world of taxes can be solved with a bit of detective work, and there is no better detective for the case than a Certified Tax Coach (CTC). By serving as your financial and tax advisor, a Certified Tax Coach can sleuth out the best opportunities for keeping more of your hard earned tax dollars in your pocket and helping you pursue your financial goals. My motto has always been "helping you **keep** more of what you make and **save** more of what you keep!"

Of course, there is no such thing as a real "tax detective," but a smart financial and tax advisor shares many qualities with the best detectives:

- A willingness to look beyond the obvious.
- A hunger for answers.
- A desire to help people.
- An encyclopedic knowledge of the law.
- Creative problem solving skills.

By being creative and looking beyond the standard or accepted way of doing things, a tax detective can uncover many opportunities that another tax professional might miss. This translates to better results for you, as you'll be able to trim expenses and put more of your pre-tax dollars to work on the things that are important to you, like your family.

Clues to Your Financial Success

A good tax coach does more than review your expenses at the end of the year and let you know how much tax you have to pay. After all, the year is over and there is not much you can do about it now. That's kind of like driving a car just using your rear view mirror! If you really want to pay less tax, you can't settle for just recording last year's history. I like to take a proactive approach, setting you up for success in years to come. To do this, a good tax coach needs to investigate your specific situation, looking for clues among existing tax laws as well as your personal needs and habits. Here are just a few things a good tax detective will investigate:

- Recent changes in tax law. Laws change all the time to reflect the ever-changing nature of the economy and other aspects of society. A good financial and tax advisor stays on top of these changes and is always looking for ways to use them to your advantage.

- Loopholes. Believe it or not, loopholes are purposely written into or left in the tax code. They are meant to be taken advantage of, and a smart tax coach will do precisely that.

- Your income. If you have a high income, you'll have a higher tax burden, but you'll also have more opportunities for side-stepping those costs, such as taking advantage of deductions you may not have been aware of or applying strategies that you never knew could apply to your situation.

- Your family. A good tax detective knows that your family can be a crucial part of developing a smart tax strategy by shifting your family income and expenses carefully.

By pulling together all of these clues, your tax coach can get a full picture of your unique situation and use that information to build a tax strategy that will really work to keep money in your pocket and help you pursue the financial path you seek for your family.

The Secret to a Successful Tax Strategy

Some aspects of income tax are non-negotiable. The amount of tax you pay for any given income bracket is set by the IRS. However, by applying the right strategies, you can impact your level of income significantly utilizing a variety of deductions, credits, etc.  Most people do not take nearly as many deductions as they can. In fact, many people don't even bother to itemize their returns, assuming that it won't be worth the trouble. As a tax professional with many years of experience, I see this all the time. It's like throwing money in the garbage can, and I haven't found anyone who enjoys doing that! A good tax detective will be able to look at your lifestyle and determine whether you have deductions or are eligible to take advantage of other tax saving strategies that can lower your tax burden.

The reason tax deductions are especially valuable is that, in some cases, they can move your expenses from post-tax dollars to pre-tax dollars, effectively reducing your overall income and saving you money on purchases you would already be making. If you're an entrepreneur or small business owner, it's likely that you're spending money after taxes that really should be tax-deductible and your tax coach should be able to identify these circumstances and set you on the right track.

The other cornerstone of a smart tax strategy is investing. Because many types of investments are tax-exempt, you can set money aside and effectively remove it from your taxable income. Not only does this save you money on this year's taxes, it also empowers you to utilize your savings for other expenses, goals, or your future retirement. The beauty of utilizing retirement strategies is the potential for tax-deferred growth.

As an example, I had a husband and wife who owned their own business. During the tax year, it became apparent that the business was going through a temporary slump, and they were running at a $60,000 loss for the year. Utilizing the opportunity to capitalize on that loss and turn it into a positive, I recommended that they each take their Traditional IRAs, which totaled approximately $90,000, and convert them to Roth IRA's. Taking into account their personal exemptions and itemized deductions, they paid ZERO income tax. Additionally, now that they both have Roth IRA accounts, they will never have to take IRS Required Minimum distributions. What's more, if they do need to take distributions from their accounts in later years, they can do so without paying any income taxes on them.

One Size Does Not Fit All

At one time or another, all of us have heard tax advice from unorthodox sources. Your brother-in-law, the mailman, the lady at the beauty parlor or the barber and, of course, a fellow coworker probably all have opinions on taxes and advice to pass along. Some of these ideas will be pure hearsay or rumors that they've picked up and passed along to anyone who will listen. Others will be illegal, whether the person telling you about them knows it or not. Some of the advice may actually be very solid, but it might not work for you the same way it did for the person telling you about it.

When you first begin to uncover the mysteries of tax law for yourself, you might be tempted to start making some changes. But just like a private investigator on the heels of a hot case, sometimes it's best to take your information to the professionals rather than acting upon it yourself.

In other words, when you hear about an exciting opportunity, bring

it up to your tax coach and see if it can apply to your case. Whether you've gotten your ideas from this book or your hairdresser, you shouldn't start making any changes to your tax strategy without the input of a professional who can understand what you're trying to accomplish and who will guide you in the right direction.

Is Your Financial Advisor a Tax Detective?

We talked earlier about the qualities that smart financial advisors and real-life detectives share. Although many tax professionals may have some of these qualities, not all of them can rightfully be called tax detectives.

You probably already have a tax professional who helps prepare your taxes for filing each year. You may also have a financial advisor who helps you look at your financial goals and make plans for your future by applying a variety of investment strategies and more. Depending on your situation, both roles might be filled by the same person, and he or she may be great at their job.

But are they tax detectives?

Can you honestly say that your financial advisor is taking the time to dig down into the clues to solve all of your tax and financial mysteries? Most of the time, tax preparers get caught in a rut. They know what's worked in the past and will continue to repeat those same actions, ignoring the clues that would lead to greater success, hoping for good results in the form of additional tax savings for you. Since you're not a tax professional yourself, you probably don't even realize that you're not getting the best tax results imaginable.

If you don't believe me, here are a few smart tax strategies that many Americans can put to use today to start shaving money off their tax bills. Every one of these is legal and has been put to good use by people just like you. As you read this list, ask yourself whether your financial advisor has ever mentioned these strategies:

- **Choosing the right business entity.** If you own your own business, you could be losing money by choosing the wrong tax entity. A pass-through corporation, like an S-Corp, provides an ideal way to trim the tax bills for some entrepreneurs.

Depending on your exact situation, the choice of business entity can also affect what benefits options you can offer, which can themselves translate into hefty tax savings as well. If you've never talked about your business entity designation before, now is the time to review your options and pick the right one.

For example, I had a client who was computer consultant. Her taxable income (after business expenses) was approximately  $200,000 per year. She was self-employed and had a few part-time employees. Each year, she was paying out a lot of money in taxes. She was very comfortable in her lifestyle and managing her finances fairly well, but she was not happy about the amount of taxes she was paying. After meeting with her and discussing her cash flow needs, it became apparent that she would be better off changing her sole-proprietorship into an S-Corporation. She paid herself a reasonable salary, which was, of course, subject to all of the normal payroll taxes. By utilizing that one strategy, she was able to reduce her personal tax bill by over $12,000 in just one year. That's over $120,000 over the next ten years of her business operations. She was ecstatic that she now had additional cash flow just from the tax savings on this one strategy that she could utilize to focus on some of her other goals.

- **Hiring family members.** By law, any child over the age of seven can be put to work at an age-appropriate task and paid fair wages. This is good news for you if you own a business. Not only does putting your kids to work teach them great life lessons, it also allows you to spend pre-tax dollars on their wages. This effectively shifts the cost of their hobbies, clothes, sports equipment or whatever else they spend money on into a business expense. You can use this same strategy for your spouse or any other family member who is financially dependent on you. Since you'd be spending money on that person anyway, shifting the money to pre-tax dollars can really trim down your tax bill. And don't forget about the grandchildren either!

- **Setting up a MERP.** A medical expense reimbursement plan is one of the best-kept secrets for paying healthcare costs with pre-tax dollars. This insurance alternative allows a business to simply reimburse an employee for medical expenses incurred. It can also be used to reimburse the cost of private health insurance. In a closely held business, you can establish a MERP for your employees, including family members, and write off 100 percent of all medical costs as a business expense on your taxes. This is still true even in a post-ACA (Affordable Care Act) world where insurance laws have changed for larger businesses.

- **Capitalizing on investment expenses.** Here's a clever idea: If you borrow money to invest, capitalize the interest on the loan as part of the basis instead of itemizing the interest as a deduction. Similarly, the trading fees  for your stocks or other investment purchases can be capitalized into the acquisition basis of the investments you are making. Your savings won't be extensive, but every dollar counts.

- **Utilizing unrealized appreciation.** Many companies offer the option to add corporate stock to your retirement plan. If this applies to you, you have an opportunity to convert some income to capital gains right after retirement. Do this by opening both an IRA and a brokerage account to hold your retirement fund. Put all of the non-stock assets into the IRA, and hold the stocks in the brokerage account. Now, just roll over enough of the stocks' market value into the IRA in order to cover your basis, and all future gains from the brokerage account will be taxed as capital gains. This is far superior to cashing out the company stock with the rest of your retirement plan and will result in more tax savings.

- **Re-categorizing real estate for depreciation.** If you've invested in real estate, you probably already know that you can write off depreciation as an expense.(At least I hope you know that.) However, houses normally devalue slowly, depreciating over a period of up to 39 years. Inside that home, on the other hand, are many features that depreciate over a different period. These include things like appliances, fences, and walkways. Every one of them can be itemized and depreciated on its own schedule and at a much faster rate if done correctly.

- **Forming a captive insurance company.** A closely held insurance company, or CHIC, is a smart solution for businesses with high levels of cash flow. If you own a company with excess profits, consider diverting them into a captive insurance company. You can put up to $1.2 million toward the CHIC in premiums each year, and that money is not subject to tax. Once it's in the CHIC, it can be rolled over into a trust. Of course, the other benefit to a CHIC is that it can be used as a real insurance company for your business, giving you a bit of padding for emergency situations.

- **Funding a spouse's IRA.** The I RS s ets a m aximum a nnual contribution limit per person, plus an added bonus amount if you have reached the magic age of 50. You can, however, fund a non-working spouse's IRA as long as your income is high enough to cover both your retirement contribution and that of your spouse. While there is no cap on the amount of income you can have in order to fund a Traditional IRA, that is not the case for a Roth IRA. You should check with a professional to be sure that your income is below the annual threshold amount, which usually changes every year. (Of course it changes every year; you know they are not going to make it easy for you to figure this stuff out.) You also want to be sure to choose the type of IRA you hold carefully and to pick the one with the best tax advantages for your particular situation.

- **Utilizing an HSA.** A health savings account allows you to set pre-tax dollars aside for medical expenses. These plans work alongside high-deductible health insurance policies, and they can be a powerful way to save money on taxes while accumulating funds to be used for your personal well-being. Best of all, money put into an HSA rolls over from one year to the next, so you don't lose any unused dollars the way you do with expensive insurance premiums. HSAs are not as popular as they once were, thanks to changes in healthcare laws that make high-deductible policies more rare, but they can still be powerful tools if you can use one.

- **Taking advantage of changes to healthcare laws.** The Affordable Care Act made many changes to the way health insurance works in the country. On the one hand, it has introduced new taxes that affect people at higher income brackets: A 3.8 percent net investment income tax is levied against all unearned income, including capital gains and real estate, and a .9 percent Medicare supplement tax is charged to anyone earning over $200,000. Fortunately, these taxes coincide with plenty of tax-reducing opportunities as well, from insurance premium subsidies for some individuals to credits for businesses that offer benefits to their employees.

- **Knowing when and how to cash out.** A good financial advisor can help you get untangled from inherited stocks or investments, the family business or other financial obligations. Sometimes the best option is cashing out. Doing so carefully can help you keep more of your inheritance and give less to Uncle Sam. For example, you might be able to use a 1031 exchange to roll funds from one account into another. If you sell a piece of real estate and carefully structure the transaction, you can use those funds to immediately invest in another similar property – hopefully, one you like a whole lot more. What's more, you can avoid being taxed on the sale. This strategy can help you reposition inherited assets that may not be working for you without taking a big hit from taxes.

These are just a few general tips and strategies that a good tax detective would be aware of. They may not be applicable to every situation, and they're a little bit more complex than what I've written here, but this should give you an idea of just how many opportunities are out there for people who are willing to look for them. By putting financial and tax knowledge to work, your tax coach can sleuth out opportunities that will work for you in your specific situation.

Is This Legal?

When people hear terms like "tax shelter" or "loophole," they sometimes get nervous. Part of the mystery of taxes is learning what's legal and what's not, and this is knowledge that any good tax detective should know. After all, a detective sides with the law, not the criminals. The reality is that a smart tax strategy is not the same as tax evasion. It's just a creative way to apply the rules and laws that  already exist to a specific situation. In fact, I am often reminded of a quote from a tax court judge, Judge Learned Hand, who said, "Anyone may so arrange his affairs that his taxes shall be as low as possible; he is not bound to choose that pattern which will best pay the Treasury; there is not even a patriotic duty to increase one's taxes." So...let the planning begin!

ABOUT THE AUTHOR

Lynn A. Schmidt, EA, CTC, CFS®, CSA, ARA

Are you overpaying your taxes? *Why?*
Do you have a plan for a comfortable retirement? *Why not?*

Do you own a business? *What keeps you up at night?*

As the Owner of Lynco Financial & Tax Services, Inc., Lynn has been in the tax planning business for over 30 years, helping her clients pursue their dreams for their financial future. She is a tax and financial problem solver who helps people find resources they may not have realized were available to them. She's kind of like a tax and financial doctor - she meets with taxpayers and business owners, takes a financial health history, does the necessary research, makes a diagnosis, and prescribes a plan of action to help clients pursue their financial goals.

Those who have trusted Lynn with their tax planning value her straightforward manner, depth of knowledge and expertise. She leads her staff as a helpful, considerate ally to clients navigating the challenges of yearly tax planning and demystifies the complexity of retirement planning. She also helps business owners keep their books and records in good order so they can pay less in taxes. By designing a personalized plan, Lynn navigates the complex tax code to help clients make smart choices about their money and finances. Her overall goal is to help business owners and taxpayers "keep more of what they make" and "save more of what they keep."

Lynn began providing accounting and tax services in 1980 after receiving a Bachelor of Science in Accounting from the University of Southern New Hampshire in Manchester. She has been an Enrolled Agent (EA) since 1997 and is also a Certified Tax Coach (CTC),

Certified Fund Specialist (CFS), Certified Senior Advisor (CSA) and Accredited Retirement Advisor (ARA).

Lynn and her husband, Don, live in beautiful Polk County, Florida. They have three children and are the proud grandparents to five. Lynn has volunteered for several years in the State of Florida as a Long-Term Care Ombudsman, working to improve the quality of life of ill or vulnerable seniors and others who live in long-term care settings, including nursing homes, assisted living facilities and adult family care homes.

Lynn can be reached at (863) 295-9895 or at Lynn@LyncoTax.com.

www.LyncoFinancial.net

www.LyncoTax.com

www.LyncoAccounting.com

CHAPTER 10

The Final Problem

Tax Planning Your Way to a Better Retirement

By Jay Malik, EA, ABA, CTC

For many workers, planning for retirement is an especially big mystery. We all know that it is important to set aside money to cover our golden years, but figuring out a good strategy for making wise investments can be a challenge. There are many retirement account options to choose from, and you can lose a lot of your hard-earned money to taxes if you are not careful. This is why it is important to establish a tax strategy to maximize the value of your retirement benefits.

Let's investigate a few of the ways you can get the most from your retirement accounts. We will put together some clues about tax strategies and investments to solve the mystery of how you can ensure a sound financial future.

Planning for Retirement

Your retirement should be one of the biggest considerations when it comes to financial planning. It takes time to build up a retirement account, and waiting too long to get started can seriously dampen your financial future. Additionally, a well-funded retirement account is important for many reasons that you might not immediately think of:

- If you are accustomed to living a certain lifestyle, your retirement account can ensure that you are able to maintain that quality of life well into old age.

- Retirement planning gives you a buffer for emergencies. As you age, you may encounter high medical expenses or other costs that you don't currently pay. Accounting for those expenses and having money to cover them are major benefits of smart retirement planning.

- For many people, retirement is a time to relax and enjoy things that they couldn't do while working. If you don't have enough money saved to accomplish these goals, though, you will have a harder time achieving these dreams.

- Retirement planning is also an important facet of estate planning. When you set aside money for your golden years, you are also setting aside money for your loved ones after you have passed away. Think of retirement planning as a strategy for establishing a financial legacy for your family.

Seeking Expert Assistance

Your retirement is too important to take into your own hands. Since multiple types of investment accounts can be involved, it helps to have a financial advisor on hand who is experienced in all of your options and can walk you through the decision making process.

It is also important to choose a financial planner who understands tax strategies and can help you create a solid plan for retirement. It doesn't matter how valuable your investments are if you lose most of your money to taxes. Knowing how to structure your retirement account disbursements is a key part of minimizing your tax burden, and this is something that a Certified Tax Coach will be uniquely qualified to help you with.

Now that we have discovered the value of retirement planning, let's investigate some of the different vehicles for retirement investments.

Afterward, we will look at some clues that can help us identify the best strategies for maximizing value without losing money to taxes.

Types of Retirement Accounts

In general, a retirement account is a special type of investment vehicle that's meant to be accessed after you have reached a specific age. Most retirement accounts have a penalty if you choose to cash out early, differentiating them from other types of investments. Since retirement accounts will usually grow over a long period, they usually rely on relatively safe investments.

The point of a retirement account is to set aside money earned while you work and grow it through investments. This makes a retirement account more valuable than simply socking away a portion of your earnings in savings. By earning interest, you can grow your wealth and create a substantial retirement income.

Many businesses offer retirement planning as an employment benefit. This may allow you to split your investment with your employer, who may match your investments while you work there. This is a beneficial arrangement for the employer as the money it invests in your retirement account is tax-deductible as a business expense. If you are self-employed, you can do the same for yourself as an employee of your own business, particularly if that business is incorporated.

Let's look at a few of the most common retirement plans and see which one might be the best match for your needs.

Pensions and Annuities

At one time, pension plans were a common benefit offered by employers. Today, they have fallen out of fashion, but some companies still offer pensions to their workers. Essentially, a pension is a retirement plan that offers you a set benefit at regular intervals throughout your retirement. You pay into the plan with every paycheck while you work at a given company. Once you have made a set number of payments, your pension is "vested," and you are guaranteed to receive retirement income from it. This security and reliability make pensions very appealing.

A pension is also one of the safest retirement vehicles because it is usually based on insurance investments rather than a high-risk, high-reward stock portfolio. If you have the opportunity to get a pension through your employer, it is usually a good idea to take it.

If you don't work for a company that offers a pension plan, you can get similar benefits from an annuity. Annuities are often sold by insurance companies, and you might be able to obtain one alongside your life insurance plan. Like a pension, an annuity provides you with a guaranteed, regular income during your retirement in exchange for regular payments into the account throughout your working life.

401(k)s

The 401(k) is so popular that it is practically become synonymous with retirement accounts. Essentially, a 401(k) is an investment account that allows you to set aside money before taxes. Your employer may match your contribution, and the contribution to your account is tax-deductible. Since you are not paying any tax on the money you invest, you will pay income tax on the disbursement when it comes time to retire.

At that point, your 401(k) will likely be worth more than the sum of your payments since it will have grown in value through years of investments. A 401(k) is not quite as safe as a pension, but it does have the potential of yielding higher rewards. You can also choose to withdraw all of it at once after retirement, allowing you greater flexibility with your retirement fund.

If you dip into your 401(k) before retirement, you'll be charged with a 10% penalty. However, there are a few exemptions to this rule. If you are facing emergency circumstances, you can take a hardship withdrawal from the account without the penalty, but you will only be able to withdraw from your own investments, not your employer's share. Otherwise, you should wait until you turn 59 1/2 before cashing out your 401(k).

Benefits of a 401(k)

A 401(k) is a great tool for reducing your current taxable income. Since a 401(k) doesn't have the same limitations as an IRA, you can pour a significant amount of money into it in any given year. This allows you to defer the tax on this income until a later date, when your overall income will be lower, effectively reducing the total cost of your tax bill.

A 401(k) is attractive from a business owner's perspective as well. Small businesses can receive a tax credit to offset the setup costs of establishing an employee 401(k), and contributions made to the account are tax deductible. These tax benefits account for the popularity of the 401(k) as a retirement plan today.

Individual Retirement Accounts

An IRA, or Individual Retirement Account, is a personal investment vehicle for setting aside retirement funds. IRAs are usually used to supplement an employer's retirement plan. IRAs are very flexible. They are not retirement plans in their own right; they are simply investment vehicles that can encompass nearly any type of investment. Real estate, stocks, bonds, and other types of investments can all be held in an IRA.

As with a 401(k), you will pay a 10% penalty if you withdraw funds from your IRA before you turn 59 1/2. You must also empty your IRA accounts by the time you turn 70 1/2; otherwise, you face a separate set of penalties.

Choose the Right Kind of IRA

There are two types of IRAs. A traditional IRA is a tax-deferred investment. You put pre-tax dollars into it, like you would a 401(k), and pay income tax on the disbursement when it is time to cash out. A Roth IRA works in reverse: you pay into it with after-tax dollars, but you pay no tax on it when you cash it out, even if it has gained value.

This makes Roth IRAs a valuable tool when it comes to tax planning. Since you can roll funds from one type of investment account to another, it is possible to move your high-earning investments into a Roth IRA. We will investigate a few ways that you can make the most from your IRAs a little later in this chapter.

There are a couple of other important things to remember about IRAs. First, you are limited to depositing $5,500 per year into the IRA. Second, if you earn more than $69,000 as an individual or $188,000 as a married couple, your traditional IRA contributions are not tax deductible. Finally, you cannot use a Roth IRA if you earn more than $110,000 per year.

Simplified Employee Pension (SEP)

An SEP is an employer-sponsored retirement plan that works similarly to an IRA. As its name suggests, it is an increasingly common alternative to the traditional pension plan.

A simplified employee pension is a profit-sharing plan that allows you to set aside up to 25% of your earnings into an individual retirement account. This lets you bypass the limitations set by both IRAs and 401(k)s while enjoying the benefits of both. If you are self-employed, you can set up an SEP for yourself and deduct the start-up costs and contributions on Schedule C, Schedule E, or Form 1065.

Social Security

If you have worked at least 10 years and paid taxes on your wages, you will qualify for Social Security payments after retirement. Social Security is a government-backed retirement program that provides income to retirees at regular intervals. You will generally receive a Social Security payment once a month, and the value of that payment will be the same each time. You can take Social Security at age 62, but you will receive a higher monthly benefit if you wait until you turn 70.

Tax Strategies for Maximum Value

Understanding your options when it comes to retirement accounts is the first step. To get the most out of your retirement planning, however, you will need to devise a smart tax strategy that will allow you to keep more of the money that you have set aside for retirement. Otherwise, you run the risk of losing a large chunk of your retirement fund to the IRS before you even get the chance to enjoy it.

The secret to smart tax planning for retirement is to monitor your income and take advantage of both taxed and tax-free accounts when each makes the most sense for your needs. Here are a few tips to keep in mind:

- Use tax-deferred investments to reduce your total taxable income today. By putting money in a traditional IRA or a 401(k), you reduce your taxable income now and thus cut your overall tax bill. When you retire, your income will be lower, meaning that you will pay less tax on that money than you would at your current income level.

- Cash out your investment accounts as you need them. It rarely makes sense to cash out all of your traditional IRAs at the same time as your 401(k). Take the disbursement from your 401(k) first, then cash out your IRAs in subsequent years.

- Roll your high-earning investments into a Roth IRA. You will need to pay tax on the deposit, but you won't pay tax on the final value of the account. If your investment is doing well, it can gain significant value in the Roth IRA, and you will receive all of that money tax-free when it comes time to cash out.

- Delay taking out Social Security if possible. Since you will need to cash out all of your IRAs in your 60s, it makes sense to empty those accounts first and use Social Security benefits afterward. Your monthly payout will be higher that way, and you won't have to add Social Security income to your IRA disbursements when tax season rolls around.

- Take out your taxable distributions, such as your traditional IRA or 401(k), in years that you have deductions to offset their costs. For example, you might still have a side business that you run in early retirement. Use business losses from that venture to offset the value of your retirement disbursement.

- If you have a pension plan or annuity, you will know how much to expect from the account every month. Plan your other disbursements accordingly, spreading them out as necessary to keep your income from being tipped into a higher tax bracket.

Special Considerations for High-Earners

In an earlier chapter, we talked about the Affordable Care Act and its effect on tax planning. There is one aspect of the ACA that is especially relevant to retirement planning: the Medicare tax assessed to investors in higher income brackets. This is a 3.8% tax charged to the passive income earned through investments.

This tax exists as a way to subsidize the cost of the Medicare expansion rolled out under the ACA. It affects only people with incomes over $250,000 per year, and it is applied only to investments worth more than $200,000.

If you would like to avoid this tax, there are a few things you can do. If your investments are in real estate, you can modify your behavior to qualify as an active participant in the real-estate business, shifting the money from passive gains to regular income. Another option would be to modify the disbursement of your retirement accounts, so that your income stays below the $250,000 threshold. Finally, you can take advantage of tax-free investments like municipal bonds in order to minimize your taxable investments.

Let's Review Our Clues:

- Retirement planning is a valuable way to secure your own financial well-being, as well as the financial legacy of your heirs.
- You should begin planning your retirement today, so that you will have enough money set aside to pay for the lifestyle you want for your golden years.
- Retirement accounts use investment vehicles to set money aside during your working years, so that it can grow in value by the time you are ready to retire.

- There are many types of retirement accounts to choose from, and some are regularly offered by businesses as an employee benefit. Some of the most common options are pensions, annuities, 401(k)s, and IRAs.

- A pension and an annuity will both provide you with a guaranteed and stable source of income throughout your retirement. An IRA or 401(k) will provide a one-time disbursement based on the value of your investment.

- There are tax benefits to setting up retirement accounts for employees, and you can also benefit from these when you are a self-employed small-business owner.

- A Roth IRA is a particularly valuable investment vehicle because it allows you to receive tax-free disbursements.

- Timing your retirement account disbursements is the key to minimizing your taxes and maximizing the value of your retirement accounts.

- High-earning individuals face additional taxes on their investment incomes, but this tax can be avoided with some careful planning.

ABOUT THE AUTHOR

Jay Malik, EA, ABA, CTC

Jay Malik is a renowned speaker and author specializing in money matters for doctors. He is a practicing Money Coach and Tax Strategist working exclusively with chiropractors, dentists, and physicians.

Jay is the inventor of "The Rich Doctor Money System," which is used by doctors all over the US to systematically manage their finances and grow their wealth. The system includes modalities to track income and expenses, reduce taxes through proactive planning, reduce debt, and build holistic wealth in a sustainable manner. Jay teaches this unique system at doctors' conferences and seminars while implementing it for his clients on an ongoing basis.

Jay manages a full-service, high-tech accounting and money-coaching firm focused on providing doctors a powerful platform to earn, retain, and grow their wealth.

He has successfully coached many doctors out of difficult financial situations, including high debt, consequences of bad investments, divorces, and dissolution of partnerships. Specializing in working with medical professionals, he is in tune with the culture and working conditions of doctors and accommodates the restrictions involved in working with them.

Jay thinks out of the box and is often critical of the accounting profession, which he says lacks creativity to serve its doctor clients. He believes that most accountants just use tax law to make money for themselves and not to save tax dollars for their doctor clients. He is quoted in CNNMoney as saying, "Whenever Congress passes a new law, they should call it an Accountant Employment Act. It increases work for accountants."

Jay is an Enrolled Agent (EA) admitted to practice before the IRS. He is an Accredited Business Accountant (ABA), a fellow of the National Tax Practice Institute (NTPI), and a Certified Tax Coach (CTC). He represents taxpayers before the IRS to ensure that they are treated fairly and pay their full legal obligation—but not one cent more.

You can reach Jay at (212) 203-9670 or jay@jaymalik.com and online at www.JayMalik.com.

CHAPTER 11

Getting Out and Keeping More

What You Need to Know About Succession Planning and Exit Strategies

By Amit Chandel, CPA, CTC, CTRS, CVA, CFE, LLM (Tax)

Succession Planning Vs. Exit Planning

With the recent buzz about baby boomer business owners preparing to leave their companies within the next few years, there can be confusion about the terminology used for this planning concept. For instance, many people believe that succession planning and exit planning can be used interchangeably when talking about owners who are in the process of leaving their businesses. However, this misconception can end up leaving you unprepared for one of the biggest financial events of your life.

In practice, succession planning and exit planning are different concepts, but ones that can work in unison to achieve the business owners overall exit objectives. Let's compare the two concepts to clear up any confusion.

Succession Planning: Focus on Transferring Leadership

Succession planning is an important concept for owners who are leaving their businesses, but this type of planning primarily focuses on the transfer of leadership and/or management from one generation to the next. This one-off approach usually identifies successors within a business and provides them with an opportunity to develop their skills and experience in order to replace the existing management at a future date. While succession planning is an important topic, it typically addresses only one aspect of a successful exit from business.

Exit Planning: The Comprehensive Approach

Exit planning, on the other hand, is the comprehensive analysis of all of the factors that impact a business owner. Exit planning addresses not only the succession aspect of leaving a business, but also a wide variety of other issues that can be important to your clients, including current and future planning with respect to their personal financial stability, their business (its value, employees, and position in the market), and their family and community. Exit planning starts from the perspective of the owner's goals and objectives in each of these critical areas, along with their current and projected resources (business value and personal and business financial resources) to identify the unique combination of strategies and steps that are most likely to allow you to reach your overall goals.

The exit planning process helps maximize the financial return, minimize tax liability, plan for contingencies, and increase the likelihood of a successful transfer of the business.

Why Exit Planning?

"In preparing for battle, I have always found that plans are useless, but planning is indispensable." Dwight D. Eisenhower (as quoted in *Six Crises* by Nixon, Richard ("Khrushchev. "1962, Doubleday)

General Eisenhower's point was that the process of creating a plan provides value because it forces the planner to consider (and make provisions for) "What if events don't proceed as planned?" A plan not only provides context and the basis for adapting to new and unanticipated events, it also provides alternatives based on assumptions about goals, objectives, and resources that may need revision.

For many businesses, their endgame is a mystery, and, like General Eisenhower, one needs to plan to remove the mystery. Business owners who create business plans are able to react more quickly to new events—events of the past few years in this economy and this world come to mind—than are those without.

According to a 2005 PricewaterhouseCoopers' survey of 364 CEOs of privately held, fast-growing companies, "65% of the respondents planned to leave their company within a decade or less, 42% within five years, and 23% in five to ten years" ("Wide Majority of Fast-Growth CEOs Likely to Move On Within Ten Years, PwC Finds," PricewaterhouseCoopers, LLP, "Trendsetter Barometer," released January 31, 2005). That could result in a glut of companies on the market, driving down valuations and giving new leverage to buyers.

If you are a baby boomer (born between 1946 and 1964), the generation following you is not nearly as big, so expect far more sellers than buyers in the marketplace. This, too, adds to the glut.

Next, even during boom times, less than half of the owners who tried to sell their business were able to actually sell (*2005 Business Reference Guide*, Tom West).

Also, unless your company is superior to its competitors because there's something about it that a buyer can use to make more money than you do (or other businesses in your industry do), that rising tide is going to lift you only as much as it lifts that glut of competitors.

If you select "wait for rising tide in the economy and the M&A market" as your exit strategy, you've lost control of the timing of your exit, the size and the terms of payment you'll receive, and even the type of buyer. Are you confident that the next boom cycle will appear when you need it?

And finally, if your reason for putting "Exit Plan" at the bottom of the list is that you believe that until the economy improves, your time and money are better spent preserving and growing business value, understand that working to create a valuable company is an integral part of any successful exit plan.

Among the benefits of exit planning are the following:

- Focus on the value-building aspects of the business that buyers seek.
- Time-sensitive accountability for each action step necessary to build value.
- Benchmark changes in business value.

Concentrating your effort on growing business value—either as a discrete project or as part of a comprehensive exit plan—affects both your ability to sell your company and the price you will be paid. In fact, your value-building plan will be inseparable from your exit plan.

Bottom line: the process of planning is what we mean by working on, not just *in*, your business. Only the planning process sets up the best opportunity to exit your business in style while minimizing the taxes.

Where other people can plan their retirement based on their employer's benefits programs, the self-employed must forge their own paths. For the small business owner, this can pose some challenges as there is no single "right way" to retire or plan the succession for the business.

Exit planning is the process through which a business owner decides what will happen to the business once he or she stops running it. Although retiring from your company or starting on a different venture might seem like a distant goal, it's important to start focusing on it right away because good exit planning often requires advance preparation and long-term financial solutions. Putting it off can cost you— from a higher tax bill to a business that fails to sell for what it's worth.

Are you like most business owners?

- A majority of closely held and family-owned businesses will change hands within the next five years; but
- Most business owners have not taken active steps to transition out of ownership.

Again, if you are like many business owners, the reasons for failing to plan may be that

- you have simply been too busy working in your business to be working *on* it—at least until now; or

- you are unsure of how to begin exit planning, who to use, or even where to begin. You can start to remove those uncertainties today.

Proper knowledge and preparation can mean millions of dollars to you when you ultimately leave your company. Start exit planning today, and you will avoid the sad (but too common) fate of T J Construction.

Years ago, Jim and Tim McCoy owned a thriving construction company. What was presumed to be a business planning meeting turned out to be a "we're getting out of business, how do we do it?" meeting. As successful as they were, they were tired of the government regulations, the changing tax codes, and the day-to -day grind of running a multimillion-dollar company.

A sale to a third party was not an option because Tim and Jim were not willing to stay on after a sale—and they had failed to develop a strong management team, which any savvy purchaser would require as a condition of purchasing the company. Transferring ownership to a group of key employees was also out of the question. None had been groomed to take on this type of responsibility, and nothing had been done to fund this type of buyout.

Both owners were too young to have business-active children, so their only option was to liquidate.

Jim and Tim's highly profitable company had little worth beyond the value of its tangible assets. After the sale of those assets, dozens of the employees lost jobs, the business disappeared, and Jim and Tim left millions of dollars on the table.

How do you avoid Jim and Tim's fate? By engaging in a proven exit planning process that you control; a process that begins by asking yourself the questions that follow below. Your exit plan will be created as you answer each of these questions affirmatively:

- Do you know your exact retirement goals, and what it will take—in cash—to reach them?
- Do you know how much your business is worth today, in cash?
- Do you know the best way to maximize the income stream generated by your ownership interest?
- Do you know how to sell your business to a third party and pay the least possible taxes?
- Do you know how to transfer your business to family members, co-owners, or employees, while paying the least possible taxes and enjoying maximum financial security?
- Do you have a continuity plan for your business if the unexpected happens to you?
- Do you have a plan to secure financial independence for your family if the unexpected happens to you?

These questions are almost misleadingly simple to ask, but to answer them affirmatively requires thought and action on your part.

Creating and implementing your exit plan is the most important business and financial event of your life.

Why Business Owners Fail to Plan

"I'm too busy working in my business to think about how to leave it. Besides, I don't know what to do—and neither do my advisors."

Sound familiar? In our experience, the primary reasons owners hesitate to begin the planning process are the following:

- You are so busy fighting alligators that you don't have time to drain the swamp. Daily demands mean all of your time and energy are spent working in the business. You have little left to work *on* the business of leaving your business.

- Owners are unaware that there is a defined exit planning process that provides a template showing them what they need to know and do in order to leave their businesses "in style."

- Most lawyers, CPAs, insurance professionals, and investment advisors—your professional advisors—don't know how to effectively work together to help you leave your business in style. If one of the professionals on your Advisory Team is a Certified Tax Coach and also/or a Certified Exit Planner, chances are good that he or she is well informed and specializes in helping owners/clients.

- Finally, many owners have a fear of the unknown—what will they do *after* they exit their businesses.

When you're ready to leave your business, you can sell it, pass it on to your family members, or simply close the doors and walk away, and there are several methods for completing any of these strategies. It's no wonder business owners often put off these decisions until the last minute.

We've come up with eight ways for owners to leave their companies.

- Transfer the company to a family member
- Sell the business to one or more key employees
- Sell to key employees using an Employee Stock Ownership Plan (ESOP)
- Sell the business to one or more co-owners
- Sell to an outside third party
- Engage in an Initial Public Offering
- Retain ownership but become a passive owner
- Liquidate

Given the right circumstances, one of these paths is the best for you. The process of determining which path is best presents an obstacle that too many owners choose to avoid. If, however, you wish to "leave your business in style," you must work through a The Seven-Step

Exit Planning Process™ (Business Enterprise Institute), which is a customized, comprehensive approach to designing and implementing a successful exit from your company. During this process, you will synthesize or harmonize your exit objectives with the characteristics and capabilities of your company as well as with the external realities of the marketplace. Exit planning uses the business owner's unique personal objectives to convert their current reality into their desired outcome.

The Seven Step Exit Planning Process

- Owner objectives
- Maximize & Protect Business Value
- Value Drivers and Cash Flow
- Ownership Transfers to Third Parties
- Ownership Transfers to Insiders
- Business Continuity Plan
- Personal Wealth and Estate Planning

Courtesy: Business Enterprise Institute

Establishing thoughtful objectives is the first step of your exit plan. Doing so well in advance of your departure gives you and your advisors the time necessary to make your goal a reality.

There's a greater mystery wrapped up in all of this as well: the financial and tax benefits of every strategy. While any option can work well for a business, not every business can benefit equally from every strategy. Solving the mystery of which tactic is more financially advantageous will put you in position to identify which strategy is best for your business, your family, and your finances. Let's look at the clues that will lead you to making the right choice.

The Importance of Financial Measurement and Management in Business Value for Exit Planning

"What makes buyers pay top dollar for your business? More to the point: f you decide to sell your business what can you do to get top dollar for your business? (*Cash Out Move On: Get Top Dollar—and More—Selling Your Business* by John H. Brown (author) and Kevin Short.)

The answer to those questions may be simple: business value. But the actions to be taken when a business owner is trying to increase business value are not as simple. One way to increase the business value is through financial measurement and management.

There are four ways to take on this task:

1. **Understand and use existing financial information:** We frequently work with successful business owners to make better use of their existing financial information, so that day-to-day activities and requirements don't overshadow broad and strategic planning. When your started your business, you had a strategic vision, and we can reconnect with that vision by regularly setting aside a reasonable amount of time to track your company's performance from an objective and quantitative perspective.

2. **Manage and reduce company debt:** Company debt is not inherently negative. In many cases, loans from outside financing sources facilitate growth more quickly than can be supported through internal financing of business opportunities. On the other hand, debt can also create additional stress and prevent growth by tying up needed cash flow. For these reasons, we often recommend that owners create strategic plans to manage the debt that supports business growth (and in turn, supports growth of business value) and to reduce debt that stifles growth and value.

3. **Implement financial controls:** Building value without specific financial goals and measures usually results in a less efficient path to success. Performance goals and limits provide the framework for successful operations and a more valuable business. As an owner develops quantifiable measures for their financial commitments and expectations, they create a more dynamic relationship between internal financial decisions and objective business value.

4. **Increase employee productivity:** Owners may feel frustrated because they feel they are too involved in day-to-day operations or have a nagging feeling that employees could demonstrate greater productivity and efficiency. Owners can work with their management-level employees to drive the productivity of these employees. When employees consistently perform at the highest levels of productivity and effectiveness, the business deserves the premium value that buyers associate with a high level of productivity.

It is important to take note of a critical mistake that can be made—a business owner's understanding of financial systems and controls may not grow at the same pace as their business grows. When a business grows, finances become more important, and that means there is more at stake, and more sophisticated measurement tools and controls are needed.

By implementing these four tasks, a business owner can add significant value to his or her business.

Measure Success

As many of you know, there are countless ways to build the value of a business using Value Drivers: (a) Creating a value-building plan is the first step an owner must take in building the business value necessary to achieve the post-exit lifestyle they desire, and (b) Tactical Planning. (According to Wikipedia, tactics are the actual means used to gain an objective, while strategy is the overall campaign plan, which may involve complex operational patterns, activity, and decision-making that lead to tactical execution. Now we start choosing tactics; in other words, we undertake the planning necessary to accomplish an owner's value goals and figure out how they will implement their decisions). Another way is by benchmarking and measuring success. This includes the following issues:

1. **Track revenue to new or returning customers or markets:** Customers represent the ultimate source of strength and success for a business. Without them, there is no business. Does your client have an accurate understanding of their customer base, and how each customer supports their business, so that the owner's strategic decisions support the future growth of his or her company? We have a number of ideas on how owners can collect and use the information they need.

2. **Measure and evaluate customer retention**: Most business owners believe that returning or repeat customers require less expense, fewer resources, and less effort to generate revenue. Similarly, third-party buyers seeking an acquisition consistently attribute higher value to a business that demonstrates healthy customer retention than to one that does not. Does your client's company systematically track, document, and report current customer retention data?

3. **Measure sales activity and effectiveness:** Whether the owner's sales activities are geared to retaining a small number of customers or to building a robust customer base, the role as the owner is to:

   • Set the unique goals and objectives for the results of sales activities

   • Communicate those goals

   • Make resources available to facilitate achievement of the goals

   • Hold people accountable when sales activity is insufficient or unsuccessful.

Do the owner's sales goals contribute to building company value?

4. **Identify critical industry metrics:** Let's look outside the company for a moment to see how it stacks up against its competitors. Every industry has its own unique rules of thumb for performance expectations. If your client's business out-performs industry norms, it is much more likely for them to develop higher value or command a higher purchase price from a buyer. Using industry metrics gives owners a set of benchmarks to compare their company's performance to other businesses with similar products, services, and customers.

5. **Define and measure success:** Driving a business toward higher value requires a constant focus on critical elements of success. A clear path to success with specific action steps and benchmarks dramatically increases an owner's ability to achieve his or her goals for growing business value.

And that's what owning and running a company is all about: building its value, so that you—the owner—can live the post-business life of your dreams. It is advisable to do a preliminary business valuation in the early stages of your exit plan to assess where you are, and where we need to be. A business valuation may seem simple, but when you have to build up the value, it can take up to 18 months. Don't let this small step put a halt on your retirement or exit.

When we talk about building value in the context of exit planning, we ask the following:

1. **What is the company's current value?**

2. **What value must the company achieve to enable its owner to reach his or her lifetime income and other exit objectives?**

3. **What tactics will you employ to close any gap between today's business value and the value you need upon exit?**

4. **How can you transfer business value most efficiently (tax and otherwise)?**

Tax Considerations for Exit Planning

How do you successfully transfer your business to a child, key employee, co-owner, or third party? We feel the most successful method is to follow a recipe that mixes, in equal measures, three key ingredients:

- The ability, experience, and dedication of the prospective new owners
- A company with strong, consistent cash flow and little debt
- A transaction designed to prevent income taxes from eroding the cash flow available to you, the seller.

It should be obvious that a business cannot be successfully transferred unless the new ownership is capable, nor can we expect the transfer to be successful if the business itself lacks the ability to provide an ongoing stream of income that can pay for the business acquisition. What may not be so obvious, however, is the corrosive effect of income taxation upon the sale of a business to "insiders"—children, key employees, or co-owners. Let's look at two key facts.

First, *your children or key employees may not have cash to buy you out.* Therefore, any sale will take many years to complete—a potentially risky prospect. Further, *all of the cash used to purchase your ownership must come from one source: the future cash flow of the business after you have left it.*

Second, without planning, the cash flow can be taxed twice. It is this double tax (usually totaling more than 50 percent) THAT spells disaster for most internal transfers. Through effective tax planning, however, much of this tax burden can be legally avoided.

Adam Smith agreed to sell his company to a key employee, John Jacob, for $1 million. This value was based on the company's annual $250,000 cash flow, which Adam historically took in the form of salary. While Adam understood that John could not pay $1 million (nor could he secure financing), he did think that he could buy out the company over a five- or six-year period, using the available cash flow of the company.

Adam's calculations were way off the mark. The time needed for a buy out was at least ten years. But why were his calculations so off base? In a word: taxes—actually in two words: double taxation. Without proper planning, this is what happens if John buys the company (and what can happen to you when you attempt to sell your business to your children or employees):

- *John receives the cash flow ($250,000 per year) and is taxed on it at a 40% rate.*

- *John pays $100,000 in taxes (40% of $250,000). This is the first tax on the business' cash flow.*

- *John pays the remaining $150,000 (net after tax) to John.*

- *Adam pays a 20% capital gains tax on the $150,000 he has received for the sale of his ownership interest, or $30,000 in taxes. This is the second tax on the original stream of income from the business.*

- *The result? The company distributed $250,000 of its cash flow, but Adam was only able to put $120,000 in his pocket.*

Without proper tax planning, you too will pay an effective tax rate in excess of 50% on the company's available cash flow used to fund your buyout. This is likely to prevent, as it did for Adam and John, a consummation of the sale of the business.

How might you avoid disaster and design your sale to minimize taxes and to maximize the opportunity for success?

1. Plan: you must have a plan that yields you a greater after-tax amount for the sale of your company. Since the cash flow of the company will not change, the key is to provide Uncle Sam a smaller slice of the available cash flow.

2. Use an experienced advisory team, usually consisting of a business attorney, CPA/CTC, and insurance or financial professional. They must understand the importance of tax sensitivity to both seller and buyer in order to make more money available to you.

3. In addition, you and your advisors must use a modest but defensible valuation for the company. Because a lower value is used for the purchase price, the size of the tax bite is reduced correspondingly. The difference between what you will receive from the sale of your business, at a lower price, and what you want to be paid to you after you leave the business is "made good" through a number of different techniques to extract cash from the company after you leave it.

Tax planning for the sale of your company to an insider takes time, planning, and expertise, but it can save a tremendous amount of money. Take time now to begin the planning process:

- Learn as much as you can about how to best accomplish the transfer of your business.

- Seek the advice of your advisory team sooner rather than later.

Act sooner rather than later. Taking action now will ensure that your business transfer recipe provides a delicious result.

Before you can understand the pros and cons of various exit planning strategies, it helps to know why some strategies are tax-preferred while others carry a high tax burden. There are a few clues to help shed some light on this issue:

- Your salary from a company is taxed as income, but the proceeds from selling the business are taxed as capital gains.

- If you gift the business or leave it to your heirs as-is, you'll end up paying gift or inheritance taxes. There are ways to sidestep these taxes, though, as we'll soon discover.

- Slowly transferring a business, either to family members or employees, will minimize the taxes for all parties involved.

With these three simple principles in mind, let's look at a few exit strategies in action, and see which one might work best for your business.

Escape Strategies for Business Owners

Over the next several years, the US economy will experience an unprecedented volume of wealth transfers. The result will be a glut of businesses for sale and downward price pressure for most privately owned companies.

To date, most analysts have focused on the inter-generational wealth transfer from the parents of baby boomers to the baby boomers themselves—a transfer that is already well underway. There is a second, less publicized and less understood transfer that also will take place over the next decade. The entrepreneurial explosion in the US over the last 30 years has resulted in record numbers of well-established small- to mid-sized private businesses with annual revenues ranging from about $1 million to $50 million. For most of the private businesses started in the 1980s and early 1990s, the owner or owners are now 50 years old and over. Just as the baby boomer demographic bulge threatens the solvency of the social security system as boomers approach retirement, the private business owner demographic bulge will seriously strain and possibly overwhelm the available supply of buyers and the support infrastructure for business transitions and transactions as these owners approach retirement. We call this the business transition tidal wave. It affords excellent opportunities for companies that learn how to effectively surf the wave.

Businesses are as diverse as the people who own them, and every company has unique needs. This means that no single succession strategy will work perfectly for every business. A freelance photographer will have a very different endgame for his company than the owner of a corporate dairy farm.

Ultimately, there are four basic options available for leaving the company that you've built: you can simply shut it down, you can sell it, you can leave it to a family member, or you can transfer ownership to an employee. Within each option, there are several strategies, with some being more tax advantageous than others.

Closing the Doors

By far the simplest solution for leaving a business is simply to walk away from it. In the case of a sole proprietorship, this can be simple. Since you and the business are one in the same, the day you stop working is the day the business shuts down. This makes good sense for many types of proprietorships that rely on your specific skills or expertise, like a freelance writing company or consulting business.

However, don't assume that just because you run a sole proprietorship that you must use this exit strategy. Your business may still be very valuable to a competitor in your field. You've spent years building up contacts and a customer base, and someone might be very interested in buying that business. Planning ahead to find a way to sell these aspects of your business to interested buyers can help create a cushion for retirement. Since there are tax benefits anyway to restructuring your sole proprietorship as an LLC, it's definitely worth considering this option now and building your business with an eye toward selling it—or at least its client base—when you decide to move on.

Bleeding a Company Dry: Lifestyle Businesses

If you're planning to close the doors on your business without passing it on to someone else, one option is to structure it as a so-called "lifestyle business." A lifestyle business exists primarily to sustain your lifestyle. Whereas other business owners might invest a large chunk of their profits back into the company to grow the business, the owner of a lifestyle business saves all profits for himself.

If you're running a corporation or partnership, this system is pretty unethical. If it's a one-man show, though, you have the right to write yourself a check for any salary you want without looking at the future of the business. While this can be enjoyable in the short term, it's not the most sustainable option. The problem is that high wages translate to high taxes, and you can stifle the growth of your company early on to prevent you from realizing the highest profits you could obtain. In other words, a lifestyle business is shortsighted; other options will be much more advantageous in the long run.

An IPO

Of the millions of companies doing business in the US, only about 7,000 are publicly traded. This doesn't stop IPOs, or "initial public offerings," from being a coveted exit strategy for some business owners. In an IPO, you essentially transfer your closely held stock over into the public stock market. In doing so, you can earn an enormous amount of money.

The problem with going public is that it's simply not an option available to most businesses. In order to secure an IPO, you'll need to capture the attention of Wall Street, and that will only happen if you're offering something really unique. It's much more likely that your business will be acquired by a large public company before your company goes public itself.

Acquisitions

In terms of selling your business, the easiest and most profitable option for you and your buyer might be an acquisition. Look at it this way: if you're selling your company to someone completely new to the business, that person will inherit all of your overhead. The cost of renting your location, paying your employees, and stocking your shelves will need to be added to the price the buyer pays for the business itself.

However, if you sell your business to a competitor, he won't have the same overhead. He already has a location and employees, so he can choose simply to take your business without all of its components. This translates to lower operating costs for him, the ability to grow his existing operation, and a higher profit ceiling for you. With this in mind, when you're ready to leave the business, approaching a few competitors can be a very wise move.

When you're implementing your exit plan, you need to consider who your successor will be. You could sell to a third party, transfer to an insider (key employee(s)), or transfer to a child.

Transferring Ownership to an Insider

Having an Employee Take Over

If the idea of selling your business to a competitor rubs you the wrong way, consider handing it over to a trusted employee instead. If you have a partnership, this might mean selling your interests in the business to one of your partners. If you're in a corporation, it might mean selling your shares to another member of the business. Whatever method you choose, there are ways to reduce the tax costs and maximize the efficiency of this option.

Leaving It to Your Family

For some people, the family business is a multi-generational legacy that can take on a life of its own. You may have established your company with the dream of passing it on to your children or grandchildren, so that their future can be secured.

Before you do this, though, it's important to make sure that it's something your heirs actually want. Having a frank conversation with your family about the business can help you determine whether anyone is excited about the prospect of taking it over, or if it's viewed as a burden that everyone is eager to escape. If you determine that some of your family does indeed want to carry on the family business, a few strategies for passing it on will minimize taxes for everyone involved.

Selling to a Family Member

One easy solution for passing the business to an interested family member is by selling it to the would-be buyer. You can owner-finance the sale, allowing the family member to buy the company over time. This turns the company into a passive income source for you while limiting the amount of money your heir needs to invest at once. It can also reduce the amount of jealousy between family members since no one will be getting the business for free.

Incidentally, this sort of owner financing can also be a good solution for selling a business to someone outside of your family, as long as you feel that you can trust the buyer.

The transfer of ownership to an insider can be a difficult and risky transfer, but it is possible.

There are three factors to why this type of transfer is risky. By creating a plan that helps to minimize your risk, you can reap all of the benefits of the transfer.

1. **Insiders have no money; therefore it is too risky to sell to them.** That's true if owners don't design a transfer strategy that puts money in the key employees' pockets as they increase the value of the company. Years in advance of the transfer, cash flow will need to be steadily and effectively built through the installation of value drivers and through careful planning to minimize taxation.

   Unless owners carefully plan to avoid it, cash flow can be taxed twice. This double tax (sometimes totaling more than 50%) can spell disaster for many internal transfers. Through effective tax planning, however, much of this tax burden can be legally avoided.

2. **Successor's management/ownership skills are untested.** If that's the case, create a written plan to systematically transition management and ownership responsibilities to the chosen successor—beginning today. The transition period, during which assumptions and the successors' skills can be tested, usually takes several years to complete.

3. **Owners lose control before being cashed out.** This is only true if owners (and their advisors) fail to implement a transfer strategy designed to accomplish the opposite: owners are cashed out before they lose control. In such a plan, owners keep control, in part through a well-designed and incremental sale of the company, over time, based upon improving company cash flow.

The following are the keys to reducing the risks of an insider transfer necessary to achieve success:

1. Plan the transfer well in advance of the desired exit date. Executing an insider transfer takes longer than executing a sale to a third party.
2. Value-building activities are just as—if not more—important to an insider transfer as they are to a sale to a third party.
3. Plan design must be tax sensitive.
4. The plan must be in writing and make advisors accountable.

Transferring Ownership to an Outsider

Selling to Strangers/Third Party

Selling a business solves two problems at once: it gives you an option for getting out from under your company, and the profits can be used as a retirement fund or starting capital for another business endeavor. In fact, selling a company can be so beneficial that some savvy entrepreneurs create businesses just to sell them later. In this regard, a company is like an investment, and the same rules of investing apply: you need to sell the business for more than you put into it in order to get a profit.

Employee Stock Ownership Plans

An ESOP is a little-known but powerful solution for slowly transferring ownership of a business over time. Basically, you set it up by establishing a trust and putting shares of the business into that trust on behalf of your employees. Your own contributions to this trust are tax deductible, and your employees pay taxes only on their disbursements. The shares are divided among employees, with those having seniority getting the largest portion. If someone leaves the company, he can sell his shares back to the business and take the money.

The thing that's nice about an ESOP is that it allows you to walk away from the business without worrying about finding a specific buyer. Once it's established, it will run itself. There are a few drawbacks to the plan, however:

- The option is limited to corporations.
- The company needs enough money to buy back the shares of an employee who decides to cash out.
- The company can become diluted through the introduction of new shares.
- An ESOP needs to be set up by a professional, and it can be a little expensive.

One way for your clients to defer capital gains tax if they own a C corporation is through an Employee Stock Ownership Plan (ESOP). Section 1042 of the Internal Revenue Code allows for the ESOP to purchase stock from the shareholder of a C corporation, and after the sale the ESOP owns at least 30% of the outstanding stock of the corporation, the selling shareholder will not be taxed on the proceeds as long as they are invested (generally speaking) in US stocks and bonds (not mutual funds).

Of course, when those replacement securities are sold, a capital gain is generated, the size of which is determined by the owner's basis in the stock sold to the ESOP. There are two ways to avoid this tax treatment:

1. Owners can hold on to those replacement securities until death when the securities receive a step-up in basis and can be sold free from any capital gain.

2. They can invest the proceeds from the sale of stock to the ESOP in high-quality floating-rate bonds. As long as these bonds are not sold, no capital gains tax is incurred. The owner can use these bonds as collateral to obtain a loan from any number of brokerage houses or other financial institutions. The interest rate for the loan will be less than 100 basis points greater than the interest paid by the bonds. The proceeds from this loan can

then be invested in a variety of stocks and bonds, or simply spent—all without any tax consequence.

When the reinvested asset is sold, a capital gain is generated, but only on the difference between the sale price and the purchase price. Combining the deferral of gain on the sale of stock to an ESOP with the purchase of long-term bonds used as collateral can mean that the business owner permanently avoids capital gains tax *(Capital Gain is defined as profits from the sale of capital assets. The gain for tax purposes is based on the gross consideration received less the basis of the ownership)* on the sale of his or her stock to the company's ESOP.

If you're interested in an ESOP, speaking with a tax professional can help you get started on the right track.

Gifting and Inheritance

When you sell a business, you pay capital gains taxes on the profits. When you gift the business, you pay gift taxes instead. Depending on your situation, one option may be more valuable than the other. Simply handing over the keys to your business can be a simple solution, but there is a better way to pass ownership on to your heirs without either of you paying much tax on the transaction.

One excellent option is a Family Limited Partnership (FLP). This allows you to slowly transfer business ownership to one or more family members. Because you transfer ownership slowly, you keep your contributions below the gift tax threshold for the year. Meanwhile, your family members will be taxed at their own individual income tax brackets, so you'll avoid inheritance tax issues.

To set up an FLP, you'll first need to structure your business as an LLC. You can speak with a tax professional or accountant about setting up the company's assets into an FLP.

Liquidation as a Last Resort

Liquidating a business is a relatively simple way to sell it, but it's certainly not a profitable option. When you liquidate, you are breaking the business down and selling its components at market value. The business itself is then shut down. Most people don't plan to liquidate, but it's sometimes inevitable.

Liquidation is often a sign of poor exit planning. A business owner who hasn't put much thought into the endgame of the company might not have made the plans required to sell it at a real profit. This leaves him needing an emergency exit from the company, often as a need to resolve debts. A bit of advance planning can save you from this problem.

Protecting Your Decision

We've examined many different methods for planning an escape from your business, but the mystery isn't entirely solved yet. Whether you're leaving it to your children or selling to a competitor, your business deserves some additional protection. There are a few insurance products that can help you feel more secure about your sale.

The first is key-person life insurance. If you're selling the business to someone over time in an owner-financed situation, you'll want some protection in case that person dies or becomes disabled before the business finishes changing hands. Life insurance can fill that need. You can also buy life insurance for yourself, so that a buyer or partner can afford to buy out your shares of a business. Since exit planning can take a long time to set up and execute, having a life insurance policy in force ensures that all of your planning isn't for naught if disaster strikes.

If you're passing your business on to just some of your children, you might want to set up a life insurance trust to provide some financial benefits to the others. This keeps things fair and will prevent strife from occurring after you're gone.

Using life insurance in conjunction with exit planning is smart business, and it's an example of the forethought that a good tax detective will put into his financial plan. No matter your current age or status of your business, it's never too early to start planning for your retirement. By deciding today what you plan to do with your business when it's time to leave, you can ensure that you take the necessary steps to achieve the best possible results.

Lets Review Our Clues:

- Business owners have unique needs when it comes to retirement, and they need to plan accordingly for the day they no longer wish to run a company.
- It's never too early to start exit planning, and most valuable exit strategies will require advanced preparation.
- Some business owners set up their companies with the plan to grow the business and sell it at a profit down the line. Whether you do this or not, looking at your company as an investment can help you make the right planning choices.
- It's financially advantageous to sell your business rather than bleed it dry through high salaries: you'll save money on taxes this way and allow your business to grow to its full potential.
- Liquidating a business is never the most profitable or advantageous option. Plan carefully in advance to avoid having to liquidate.
- Selling your business to a competitor can yield you the highest profits.
- You're more likely to be acquired by another company than to go public with your own company, so plan accordingly.
- There are tax-preferred methods for slowly transferring ownership of a business to your employees or family members, so start putting them to work early to get the best results.
- Insurance products can be used in conjunction with your succession strategy to ensure that your plan is safeguarded against disaster.

There's a simple checklist to guide you through that process.

As you read through the checklist, ask yourself if this is a process you can orchestrate yourself, or if you just might need an advisor skilled in Tax & Exit Planning to design, facilitate, and direct the process.

The Owner's Checklist

1. Establish your goals. Start with the Big Three:

   a. How many dollars do I need from the transfer of my business to achieve financial independence? Or, put another way, what is the annual income I (and my family) need *and* want in order to exit?

   b. How many more years must I stay in my business to reach that value and sustainable income level?

   c. Can the successor I envision pay me that value, or should I consider other buyers?

   Now list all of the other goals you may have for yourself, your business, and your family upon your exit. The list might include the following: maintain your company's culture or your legacy, benefit loyal employees, and/or preserve family harmony.

2. Inventory your existing resources.

   a. What is the current value of your business and non-business assets?

   b. What is your company's current cash flow?

3. Calculate the size of the gap between the current value of your assets and the asset value you need in order to provide financial independence. Doing so involves a few more calculations:

   a. Given your risk tolerance, what is a reasonable rate of return that you can expect on your investments?

   b. Based on actuarial tables, how long can you and your spouse be expected to live?

    c. Based on your current spending habits and on the lifestyle you wish to enjoy after you leave your company, how much money do you need each year after you exit your business?

    d. Based on your company's historical growth rates and future prospects, how quickly can you expect cash flow to grow?

    e. What tax rate are you likely to pay on the sale or transfer of your ownership interest?

Armed with that data, calculate the amount of money that you will need from the sale (or transfer) of your company to support the lifestyle you desire for the duration of your post-business life.

So far, pretty simple, right? Now it gets more involved.

4. Using all of the information you have gathered, create a series of actions that will achieve the goals you have set. Each action should contribute to:

    a. Growing value,

    b. Reducing taxes, or

    c. Minimizing business risk.

Assign each action to a responsible party—one of your advisors, perhaps?—who you will hold accountable for accomplishing it within a reasonable amount of time.

5. Make sure that the plan you create is flexible enough to adapt to changing circumstances, keeps you in control of your company until you are completely cashed out, and minimizes risk of failure.

6. If you plan to transfer your company to key employees or children, remember that they do not have enough cash to purchase your ownership. Figure out how to a) get them the cash required, b) minimize risk, and c) maximize the value you will receive, all while retaining control until you achieve *all* of your goals and aspirations.

If transferring to children, create a way to manage the transfer to one or more children that keeps everyone in the family happy and does not put the business at risk.

7. Don't forget the Tax Planning Advisor/Coach. Design these transfers in a tax-effective manner, understanding that good tax planning can increase proceeds to you by 30% or more.

8. If you plan to sell your company to a third party, make sure all value drivers (those characteristics buyers look at in an acquisition) are present and working effectively. Make certain you and your company is 100% ready to go to market and be sold for the net proceeds (not sale price) you need—before you go to market. (Before proceeding, you might re-acquaint yourself with the list of Deal Killers).

9. Consider and plan for the events that could happen to you prior to your planned exit date (such as death) and create mechanisms to protect both your business and your family.

10. Make sure that your estate plan works consistently with the plan you've created to transfer your business.

I think that about covers it. Well, except for the facts that

a. Each of your goals should have its own set of action items. (Plans usually involve about three dozen or more.)

b. Most strategies to grow value involve creating performance standards for management and others that are unique to each owner's goals and business.

c. Contingency plans aren't a whole lot of fun to create, but with or without them (with a poorly considered plan or without a plan at all), your business and your family's financial security are on the line.

d. You already have a full-time job running your company.

So, who is going to create the plan required to achieve *your* objectives? And who is going to execute that plan?

I suggest that you find a Tax Planning Advisor/Coach skilled in exit planning and hand him or her the list above, and they'll know what to do.

ABOUT THE AUTHOR

Amit Chandel,
CPA, CTC, CTRS, CVA, CFE, LLM (Tax)

Mr. Amit Chandel has practiced as a Certified Public Accountant for over 20 years at Focus CPA Group Inc. where he is the principal. Prior to that, he spent time in various corporate-level accounting roles where he found his passion of helping business owners achieve their financial goals and dreams. He helps his business owner clients grow their businesses and plan for the single, most critically important financial event of their lives—the transition out of their business. He also helps his clients to navigate the complex tax code and advises them on strategies tailored to their individual situations. As a Certified Tax Coach, he is in a position to advise his clients to minimize their taxes by using the tax code year after year.

Amit is a graduate of Cal State Long Beach with a Bachelor of Science degree in Accounting, and of Washington School of Law with an LLM in Tax. He is also a Certified Tax Resolution Specialist.

You can reach Amit at (562) 281-1040 or (714) 784-0153 or by sending him an email at achandel@focuscpa.com.

www.focuscpa.com

CHAPTER 12

Estate Planning
The Mystery of the Ghost Tax

By Anthony J. Amatore, CTC

How to Reduce or Eliminate Estate Tax by Planning Ahead

The saying goes that there are just two guarantees in life: death and taxes. Unfortunately, even the very best tax planning throughout your lifetime cannot protect you from paying tax *after* you've died. Estate tax may be one of the biggest mysteries in the tax code, but making estate tax reduction as high a priority as avoiding income taxes will help ensure that you're not overpaying from the grave.

Piecing Together Estate Tax

What are estate taxes?

Estate taxes are quite different from ordinary income tax. Perhaps this is why most tax professionals treat this area as a mystery. These taxes are also quite different from probate expenses, which occur when the deceased (also known as the decedent) dies without a will or a revocable living trust.

Federal estate taxes are not cheap. Historically, the rates range from 45 to 5%, and generally they must be paid in cash within nine months after you die. Since very few estates have the cash needed to pay these taxes, it often leaves the heirs forced to liquidate assets (such as selling the family home or family business) just to be able to afford to pay the tax. But when you plan ahead, you can greatly reduce or even eliminate estate taxes.

Who has to pay estate taxes?

Your estate will have to pay federal estate taxes if your net worth at time of death is more than the amount prescribed by Congress. In 2013, the threshold was $5,250,000 and the estate tax was 40%. At the start of 2014, they were $5,340,000 and 40% respectively.

In addition, some states have their own death or inheritance tax, so your estate could be exempt from federal tax and still have to pay state tax. With most of the strategies in this book, it is important to also plan to reduce state taxes—because they add up!

In order to understand the tax strategies discussed in this chapter, it is helpful to first understand how estate tax is calculated.

First, you must calculate the net value of your estate. To determine the current net value, add your assets, and then subtract your debts. Include your home, business interests, bank accounts, investments, personal property, IRAs, retirement plans, and death benefits from your life insurance.

When adding your assets, it is important to use accurate valuations. The risk of being audited on estate tax returns is extremely high. In fact, the IRS audited over half of all estate tax returns filed with net assets valued up to $10 million. You'll need to include all real estate you own as well as stocks and bonds, other investments, cash, and various personal property (even your clothing and furniture).

Once you've figured your total assets, you are allowed to make certain deductions. These include funeral costs, costs to administer your estate, mortgages, and other debts, and promises you've made to your spouse or charities.

Last, you must add any gifts that were made prior to 1976 (we'll talk more about gifts later in this chapter). However, you do get to deduct any gift taxes that were paid after 1976.

Your estate may be subject to an additional "generation skipping" tax. This happens when there are transfers in the estate to skip people in your life who are more than one generation below you when transfers exceed $1,000,000.

Estate Tax Reduction Strategies

While there are many strategies available for estate tax planning, this chapter will focus on three specific methods for eliminating or greatly reducing this "post-death" tax. First, if you are married, using both spouses' estate tax exemptions can dramatically reduce estate tax that is due when the first spouse passes away. Second, removing assets from your estate before you die effectively reduces the net value of the estate subject to the tax. Last, purchasing life insurance to replace donations from your estate to charity can help reduce your taxable estate or cover remaining estate taxes, so your heirs are not forced to liquidate assets you intend to "keep in the family."

Using Both Spouse's Exemptions

One of the biggest advantages to estate tax planning is your ability to leave your spouse an unlimited amount without having to pay estate tax. This advantage is now more widely available to married same-sex couples in the United States with the new Defense of Marriage Act provisions. As long as your spouse is a US citizen, and your marriage is recognized in the United States, you can leave him or her an unlimited amount; this effectively removes these assets from your estate. Unfortunately, the planning cannot end with this strategy as problems can arise when the second spouse dies.

Once the second spouse dies, their own exemption amount of $5,250,000* ($5,340,000 in 2014) can be used to reduce the value of their estate. In addition, the spouse that is last to die can use any of his or her deceased spouse's exemption, which has not been used previously, as long as he or she does not remarry. The problem arises when a new marriage occurs. Should the surviving spouse also outlive his or her second spouse, he or she would no longer be able to use the deceased spouse's unused exemption amount.

In addition, when using the spousal exemption, the first spouse has no control over how their share of the estate is distributed as he or she is essentially giving it all to the surviving spouse.

One way to resolve this issue is to plan ahead, so both spouses can use both of their exemptions and control where their assets go after death. By forming a living trust that splits your estate into two trusts, each spouse can use his or her full exemption, which can reduce your taxable estate and pass the majority of your assets on to your loved ones.

One last benefit is that by splitting the trust, both spouses can take advantage of the full exemption available to them, but the assets in both spouses' trusts can be available to either spouse.

Married couples with estates of all sizes can use this strategy to reduce or even eliminate estate tax in an efficient way.

Removing Assets from Your Estate

Since estate taxes are based on the net value of your assets when you die, one easy way to reduce this is to decrease the size of your estate before you die. Essentially, this means spending some of it. Most likely, you know who should have your assets after you die. If you can afford it, why not make some gifts now and save estate taxes? It can be very satisfying to see the results of your gifts—something you will obviously miss out on if you wait until you die.

When determining the best assets to gift, consider using assets that are increasing in value. These types of assets are optimal because any future appreciation will not affect your estate.

While this strategy can help reduce your estate tax, it may not help your heirs avoid their own tax when they sell the assets. This is because assets that you gift maintain your cost basis (what you paid for them), so when they are sold, your recipients may be subject to capital gains tax on the difference between the sales price of the property and your cost basis. In the long run, while you may not be able to prevent *all* tax, capital gains rates are only as high as 20%, which is still less than half of the estate tax at 40% if you kept the assets until you die.

You might also consider making annual tax-free gifts that are below the gift tax exemption. Gifts with a value of less than $13,000 each year per recipient are not subject to gift tax. You can do this for as many people as you wish.

This simple method can also be a good way to fund medical or educational expenses: as long as you make gifts for medical or educational expenses by paying the provider directly, you can use this method to transfer an unlimited amount out of your estate.

Last, an unlimited amount is also exempt from gift tax for transfers that are made to a charity—so be generous! It may help you pay a lot less in tax!

There are other ways to reduce the value of your estate by removing assets. However, the following ideas are what is known as "irrevocable," meaning you cannot change your mind at a later time.

Irrevocable Life Insurance Trust

You might consider placing your life insurance policy inside of a trust. You can remove the value of your insurance from your estate by making an Irrevocable Life Insurance Trust (ILIT) the owner of the policies. As long as you live three years after the transfer of an existing policy, the death benefits will not be included in your estate.

Placing your life insurance inside of an ILIT means the trust becomes the beneficiary of the policy. This gives you the opportunity to keep the proceeds in the trust for years, allowing for distributions over time to your spouse, children, or other heirs. One popular feature of the ILIT is that your trust can contain spending provisions, so that the funds are protected from creditors, you prevent irresponsible spending, and a spouse or other unintended family members can be kept away from this money.

Qualified Personal Residence Trust

Since your home is often a substantial value in your estate, you may consider placing your home inside of a Qualified Personal Residence Trust (QPRT). A QPRT removes your home from your estate without forcing you to stop living in the home. You are allowed to transfer your home to a QPRT for a period of time, usually 10 to 15 years. During this time, you continue to live there. When the trust term is up, the home transfers to the trust beneficiaries. Want to stay there longer? You can even make arrangements to pay rent. Should you die before the trust term ends, your home will be included in your estate, just as it would without this strategy. But the benefits of using the QPRT go beyond removing this asset from your estate.

A QPRT "leverages" your estate tax exemption. Since your children will not receive the house until the trust ends, its gift value is reduced. The tax advantage of the QPRT stems from the fact that when the residence is transferred into the trust, you do not pay gift tax on the full market value of the property. Instead, the gift is based on the value of the property, reduces by the interest you have retained by continuing to live in the house.

For example, if your personal home has a market value of $1,000,000, and you are in the 50% marginal tax bracket, the estate tax could be as high as $500,000 (assuming your estate exceeds the exemption amount). If instead you leave your residence to your heirs by placing it inside of a 15-year QPRT, so long as you survive until the end of the trust term, the tax result is much different. Rather than paying tax on the full $1,000,000, you would pay a 50% tax on the value ($1,000,000) minus the value of the 15-year interest you retain in the transaction. At a 4% interest rate, this value is a little over 41% of the total value of the property. This means the value of the interest passing to your heirs is only about 59% of the total, creating tax savings of over $250,000! Use of this strategy also leaves much more of your exemption available for other assets, reducing even more of your overall estate tax.

Grantor Retained Annuity Trust

Similar to a QPRT is a Grantor Retained Annuity Trust (GRAT). This type of trust strategy allows you to transfer an income-generating asset like stocks, real estate, or business into a trust for a set period of time. This effectively removes the value of the asset from your estate— yet, you can continue to receive income. If your income is a consistent amount, the trust is known as a GRAT; if the amount fluctuates, the trust is known as a Grantor Retained Uni Trust(GRUT).

When the trust ends, the asset inside the trust will go to the beneficiaries. Since they will not receive it until then, the value of the gift is reduced. If you die before the trust ends, some or all of the assets may be in your estate.

Family Limited Partnership or LLC

If you're looking to remove the value of a family business, farm, or real estate from your estate, a Family Limited Partnership (FLP) or LLC may be a solution. Again, you reduce the value of your estate by transferring these assets, but you can still keep some control. The FLP or FLLC also protects the assets from lawsuits and creditors, providing valuable asset protection.

Similar to the QPRT or GRAT, you set up an LLC or FLP and transfer the business assets into it. In exchange, you receive ownership interests. Though you have a fiduciary obligation to other owners, you control the LLC (as manager) or FLP (as general partner). You can give ownership interests to your children, which removes value from your taxable estate. These interests cannot be sold or transferred without your approval, and because there is no market for these interests, their value is often discounted. This lets you transfer the underlying assets to your children at a reduced value, without losing control.

Charitable Remainder Trust

Finally, a Charitable Remainder Trust (CRT) allows you to reduce your current income taxes as well as estate taxes. The CRT lets you benefit a charity that has special meaning to you and turn highly appreciated assets (such as stocks or investment real estate) into lifetime income without paying capital gains tax when the asset is sold. With a CRT, you transfer the asset to an irrevocable trust which removes it from your estate. You also get an immediate charitable income tax deduction.

The trust can sell the asset at market value, paying no capital gains tax, and reinvest in income-producing assets. For the rest of your life, the trust pays you an income. Since the principal has not been reduced by capital gains tax, you can receive more income over your lifetime than if you had sold the asset yourself. After you die, the trust assets go to the charity you have chosen. Most taxpayers opt to use the tax savings created with the charitable deduction to purchase life insurance for their beneficiaries.

Consider Purchasing Life Insurance

Speaking of life insurance, buying life insurance can be an inexpensive way to replace an asset given to charity or pay remaining estate taxes. The cost, of course, depends on your age and health. When you have a new policy, you should consider having an ILIT purchase the policy, so that the benefits are kept out of your estate.

Let's Review Our Clues for Reducing Estate Taxes:

If Married, Use Both Exemptions

Living Trust with Tax Planning

• Uses both spouses' estate tax exemptions, doubling the amount protected from estate taxes and saving a substantial amount for your loved ones

Remove Assets From Your Estate

Make Annual Tax-Free Gifts

- Simple, no-cost way to save estate taxes by reducing the size of the estate.

- $13,000 ($26,000 if married) each year per recipient (amount tied to inflation).

- Unlimited gifts to charity and for medical/educational expenses paid to provider.

Transfer Life Insurance Policies to Irrevocable Life Insurance Trust

- Removes death benefits of existing life insurance policies from estate.

- Included in estate if you die within three years of transfer.

Qualified Personal Residence Trust

- Removes home from estate at discounted value You can continue to live there.

Grantor Retained Annuity Trust / Grantor Retained Uni Trust

- Removes income-producing assets from estate at discounted value.

- You can continue to receive income.

Limited Liability Company / Family Limited Partnership

- Lets you start transferring assets to children now to reduce your taxable estate.

- Often discounts value of business, farm, real estate, or stocks.

- Can protect the assets from spouses, creditors, and future lawsuits.
- You keep control.

Charitable Remainder Trust

- Converts appreciated asset into lifetime income with no capital gains tax.

- Saves estate taxes (asset out of estate) and income taxes (charitable deduction).

- Charity receives trust assets after you die.

Buy Life Insurance

Irrevocable Life Insurance Trust

- Can be an inexpensive way to pay estate taxes and/or replace charitable gifts.

- Death benefits are not included in your estate.

ABOUT THE AUTHOR

Anthony J. Amatore, CTC

Anthony Amatore is a graduate of Youngstown State University. He is an Accountant, Certified Tax Coach, Tax Practitioner, and Estate and Financial Planner, and he has the ability to practice in all 50 states. He is also approved to represent clients in the Local Probate Courts. Anthony has been honing his skills for 30-plus years, helping his clients plan for today and for the future.

The diversity in Anthony's business experience and his expertise in tax planning have allowed him to provide the most comprehensive services to his clients. He has assisted many start-ups in getting off the ground and growing into admirable businesses.

Whether holding client meetings during a telephone conference, online video conference, or in person, he has truly shown that he cares for his clients.

Anthony sends educational emails to all his clients weekly, does quarterly planning seminars, and supplies appropriate information to all his clients to help them better understand their tax dilemmas. He stays in touch with a typical client 72 times a year. For that, many of his clients have given him the name that Anthony is most proud of, the title of "Trusted Advisor."

Anthony and his wife Traci have been married for 25 years, have three children, and work and reside in Canfield, Ohio. He and his wife are very active in their community, supporting various school events for their children and numerous charities, as well as his alma mater, Youngstown State University.

Anthony is the current Treasurer of Sheperd of the Valley Nursing Homes, sits on the board of a Medical School in Northeastern Ohio, and is a member of the Youngstown-Warren Regional Chamber of Commerce and The National Association of National Tax Preparers. Being a Certified Tax Coach leads him to challenging and interesting endeavors daily.

Anthony can be reached at 330-533-0884 or cfpinyo@gmail.com.

www.ajamatore.com

CHAPTER 13

Making Taxable Income Disappear

The Domestic Production Activities Deduction

By Pat O'Hara, EA, CTC

T he economy is changing, and more small businesses are emerging to fill the void left by corporate downsizing. Entrepreneurs are using their skills to add value to products and services and find ways to compete in the global marketplace while maintaining profitability. One of the most important business strategies that is often overlooked is how to plan for and manage tax liability. Small-business owners should never forget the maxim, "A dollar saved in tax is worth more than a dollar earned."

How can business owners find out what little-known deductions can offset their tax liability? It is worthy of some investigation. I often remind my clients that Congress put deductions, credits, and loopholes in the tax code to promote small business because it is the foundation of our economy. One of the most misunderstood deductions is the Section 199 "Domestic Production Activities Deduction," or DPAD for short. If you have never heard of this deduction, you are not alone. I am always surprised when colleagues tell me they have never heard of it because this deduction even has its own line on the front page of the tax return. It is equally disturbing when I learn that a taxpayer has either been told they don't qualify for the deduction, or that it is too time consuming to claim and is not worth pursuing. How could potentially lowering your taxable income by 9% not be worth pursuing? A good tax detective will inspect your business to see if this deduction can be spied out for you.

I will admit that this deduction is a little intimidating, but it gets much easier to understand once you get past the bulky terms and acronyms. Fortunately, there are Certified Tax Coaches that specialize in this area of tax planning that can help you determine if your business is eligible for this deduction, show you how to properly structure your business transactions so you meet all of the requirements, and determine the best method to calculate the deduction to maximize your savings. Let's examine the case of the missing DPAD.

Congress Created This Deduction to Promote Small Businesses

The Domestic Production Activities Deduction (DPAD) was added to Section 199 of the tax code as part of the *American Jobs Creation Act of 2004* as a way to ease the tax burden on domestic producers and manufacturers. Congress created this incentive for goods to be "Manufactured, Produced, Grown, or Extracted (MPGE)" in the United States while promoting employment. Aside from traditional manufacturing, it also promotes construction, engineering, and architectural services performed in the US for construction in the US. Qualifying for the deduction requires the business to pay W-2 wages rather than subcontracting out the labor. The deduction may be taken by individuals, partnerships, corporations, and even some trusts and estates, and it allows for the exclusion of income from taxation.

Starting in 2009, the deduction increased to 9% of qualifying production activities income. In simple math terms, if your qualifying net income is $100,000, your deduction is $9,000. For a taxpayer in the 25% marginal tax bracket, this equates to tax savings of $2,570 or more. The most difficult part of claiming DPAD is determining what income qualifies for the deduction. This task is best left to your Certified Tax Coach. Your concern should be focused on what to do with all of the money you are going to save from claiming this deduction this year and every year going forward.

What makes DPAD so important for tax planning is that, for most small-business taxpayers, the deduction is an adjustment to income on their personal income tax return. This deduction lowers the taxpayer's adjusted gross income (AGI). We sometimes call this an above-the-line tax deduction. Marginal tax rates, Alternative Minimum Tax (AMT), the new Net Investment Income Tax (NII), and many tax credits are affected by AGI. In short, lowering AGI on the personal return can yield big savings by lowering the marginal tax rate and increasing eligibility for certain tax credits. This deduction becomes even more valuable as tax rates for individuals continue to rise.

The Basics of DPAD

We said earlier that the basics of this deduction are qualifying income from goods Manufactured, Produced, Grown, or Extracted (MPGE) in the United States while promoting employment. These activities result in creating Qualified Production Property (QPP). This property can be leased, rented, licensed, sold, or exchanged to qualify. MPGE includes developing, improving, and creating QPP out of raw materials, scrap, salvage, or junk, or by changing the form and function of an article. These can be items that are produced on a factory assembly line or are handmade. The DPAD applies to farming activities such as cultivating soil, growing crops, raising livestock, and repurposing waste products. In terms of salvage operations, it could be something as simple as shredding old tires and creating a new form of raw materials for further manufacture. It may also apply to fishing and to mining for minerals and other natural resources. Even qualified films or TV productions, electricity, natural gas, or potable water produced in the US qualify.

DPAD also includes construction, as well as engineering and architectural services performed in the US for construction projects in the US. This means that most residential and commercial contractors, subcontractors, and developers of any original construction or capital improvement projects may qualify for this deduction. We are talking about carpenters, electricians, plumbing and heating contractors, masons, excavators, and all other building trades involved in constructing or improving real property. The determination of qualifying activities is performed on an item-by-item basis, which essentially means that for purposes of claiming the deduction, each qualifying job must be looked at separately. Although there are many rules, a Certified Tax Coach is in the best position to determine if you qualify.

Does Your Business Qualify for the Deduction?

The range of businesses that qualify for DPAD is much wider than most people think. One might think that this deduction only applies to big manufacturing businesses, but with a skillful understanding of the tax code, legislative intent, and court cases, many other businesses that make or add value to things may also claim this tax-saving deduction. What is important to note is that the courts seem to be taking a very broad interpretation on the application of this deduction based on leg-islative intent, provided the taxpayer meets certain tests under the law. In my practice, we apply this deduction to a variety of small businesses including building contractors; farming and florists; businesses that make furniture, wine, or cheese; wholesale food-service operations; print shops; and recycling operations that transform or repurpose scrap materials. Although professional services would not generally qualify, some aspects of their services may. Examples could be an eye doctor who custom-makes eye wear, grinding lenses and assembling them into frames. It may also apply to a compounding pharmacist who has to mix or transform medications for special use.

Recent court cases have expanded the interpretation of what types of activities qualify for this deduction. One of the most notable cases involved a business that made custom gift baskets.[1] The company basically took items that are normally sold by other retailers and packaged them into gift baskets and resold them. In short, the value of the completed basket was higher than the cost of its contents. The court found that this creation of value, or the process that created it, is what qualifies it for DPAD. A similar ruling by the IRS Office of Chief Counsel also noted that photo processing in a retail pharmacy qualifies when the taxpayer uses his own raw materials (photo paper, ink, and other chemicals) to produce a different tangible product in form and function.[2] In the area of construction, the courts found that a substantial renovation of property qualified because it materially increased the value of the property and substantially prolonged its useful life.[3]

Who Is Taking the Deduction?

Federal statistics show that two thirds of businesses taking this deduction are in the manufacturing sector. Manufacturing generally refers to building personal property for resale—items such as clothing, furniture, computer components, jewelry, and so on. The second-largest sector taking the deduction is information technology, particularly with the development of computer software, including packaged software, gaming software, and some other software that is available through download.[4] This deduction may also be available to the growing segment of app developers.

Keep in mind that the reason manufacturing and IT companies represent the majority of this deduction is because these industries are often controlled by large conglomerates. Small businesses that currently don't qualify probably could with some simple restructuring. It is important to note that many non-manufacturing small businesses may benefit most from this deduction: they have the advantage of using much simpler methods to calculate DPAD, and generally, if using a cash-basis accounting system, may not have to capitalize costs as required by larger businesses.

The construction industry may be the biggest benefactor of this deduction in coming years as residential and commercial construction increases. Generally, all of the capital costs of new construction, associated excavation, engineering and architectural planning qualify for the deduction provided they occur in the US. Many capital improvement projects also qualify. These include improvements that become structural components of the property, increase the property's value, change its purpose, or extend its useful life. On the contrary, activities that solely include maintenance and repair would not qualify.

Most income from farming and agricultural activities also qualifies for the deduction. This includes most of the income reported on Schedule F, such as crop revenue, other farm-related income, and gains from the sale of raised breeding, dairy, or draft livestock. Dairy farms, or their subsidiaries that process milk products, also qualify. Farms that raise cattle for slaughter and conduct their own butchering activities such as grinding, smoking, or curing meats may also qualify.

Food Service Industry Exception

One of the exceptions to DPAD is the food service industry. The gross receipts of food and beverages prepared at a retail establishment don't qualify for DPAD. However, a food service that prepares food and sells it wholesale may be eligible to take the deduction. For example, we worked with a caterer who prepared pre-packaged sandwiches and salads that were sold to convenience stores for resale. The income from this activity qualified for DPAD, but their regular catering activities generally didn't. We had a similar case with a pizzeria that had contracted with a local school to produce pizzas for resale to students. The income from selling the pizza to the schools qualified for DPAD, but the pizzas sold out of their shop didn't. Similarly, the bakery selling its products on site didn't qualify, but items that were shipped out to retailers were eligible for the deduction. Some food service businesses are restructuring to have one business prepare food at one location and then sell it wholesale to a subsidiary for resale at another location.

Paying Wages

The requirement of paying wages is the deciding factor in claiming DPAD. The deduction is limited to 50% of allocable wages. These are wages that can be allocated to the domestic production gross receipts (DPGR). These must also be wages that are subject to employment taxes, which means that wages paid to minor children that are exempt from employment taxes, or wages paid in commodities (a great loophole for farmers), don't qualify for purposes of DPAD.

Many small businesses don't pay wages and prefer to use subcontractors or family members. DPAD can be a way to offset the cost of putting employees on payroll. Adding formal employees to the business may help a business grow and even provide for an exit strategy as the small-business owner turns the day-to-day operation over to employees. Shifting income to family members in a lower tax bracket is a solid strategy. Paying wages to a spouse creates eligibility for a Section 105 Medical Reimbursement Plan, and, more importantly for the otherwise non-working spouse, wages can also create eligibility for Social Security, Medicare, and survivor's benefits.

Terms You Need to Know

The following terms define the rules for determining the DPAD. They are big, bulky, and sometimes annoying to read out loud—but the tax savings are generally well worth the effort.

Qualified Production Activities Income (QPAI) is the amount equal to Domestic Production Gross Receipts (DPGR) less the allocable Cost of Goods Sold (COGS) less other properly allocable direct and indirect costs.

Domestic Production Gross Receipts (DPGR) are the gross receipts derived from the active conduct of a trade or business; construction of real property; the active conduct of an engineering or architectural service trade or business with respect to the construction of real property; and/or the subsequent sale or lease of Qualified Production

Property (QPP) to the taxpayer who originally manufactured, produced, grew, or extracted (MPGE) the qualified production property (QPP) within the US.

Qualified Production Property (QPP) is considered tangible personal property, computer software, and sound recordings.[5] The definition for DPAD purposes may be different from state law. For instance, tangible personal property does not include land, buildings, inherently permanent structures, land improvements, or oil and gas wells and infrastructure. For DPAD purposes, machinery, printing presses, transportation equipment, office equipment, refrigerators, grocery counters, testing equipment, display racks, and shelves and signs contained in or attached to a building are tangible property.

Calculating the Deduction

The DPAD involves some very simple math. All that needs to be done is to calculate 9% of Qualified Production Activities Income (QPAI). QPAI is computed by deducting the cost of goods sold, and direct and indirect expenses from DPGR. Remember that these terms may sound menacing, but they just represent special definitions that carry special rules. A Certified Tax Coach can show you how they work.

The tax code provides three different methods for calculating the deductions. Small-business owners have the advantage of being able to choose any of the three methods, and the taxpayer can change methods each year, choosing the one that yields the highest deduction. I tend to believe that the smaller the business, the easier it is to take this deduction.

- The Small Business Simplified Overall Method (SOM) is for taxpayers with less than $5 million in average annual gross receipts, some farmers, and taxpayers eligible to use the cash basis of accounting.[6] The SOM allows the taxpayer to allocate direct and indirect costs based on the ratio of DPGR and non-DPGR. This is the easiest method for small businesses.

- The Simplified Deduction Method (SDM) is for taxpayers with less than $100 million in average annual gross receipts or $10 million in total assets.[7] The SDM requires that the taxpayer determine the proper amount of costs of goods sold to allocate to DPGR and then apportion other costs between DPGR and non-DPGR. This method requires a little more research, but can sometimes yield a higher deduction than the SOM.

- The Section 861 Method may be used by any taxpayer and is the most complex method as it requires the taxpayer to specifically identify and trace the cost of goods sold (COGS) to different classes of income, and then allocate its other deductions to relevant classes of income and expenses. Unless required by law, only businesses with the most sophisticated cost accounting systems would use this method. It is a very detailed item-by-item analysis of qualifying revenue and job costs. In some cases, this method may yield the highest deduction.

Examples of Applying the Different Methods

A printing company provides a variety of services, including printing simple copies, custom cutting, folding, and, at times, binding materials. Activities that involve a process that changes the form and function of the paper, such as cutting, folding, or binding, qualify for the deduction—provided all other tests for the deduction are met. For the purpose of this example, let's say that a company's gross receipts for the year were $1,000,000, of which $850,000 involved production processes beyond simple copying. The cost of goods sold was $250,000 and the indirect costs were $100,000.

Using the Small Business Simplified Overall Method (SOM), we see that the production revenue was 85% of the total revenue. We would use the 85% of the gross receipts less 85% of COGS, less 85% of indirect costs to get our Qualified Production Activities Income (QPAI). This would be $850,000 less $212,500 of costs of goods sold ($250,000 times 85%) less 85,000 in direct costs ($100,000 times 85%), which would equal QPAI of $552,500. The deduction would be 9% of $552,500, or $49,725, subject to the 50% of W-2 wages rule.

Using the Simplified Deduction Method (SDM) we would take the $850,000 in production revenue and subtract the actual cost of goods sold, say $250,000, less the actual allocable indirect costs, say $25,000. This would give us QPAI of $585,000. The deduction would be 9% of $585,000, or $52,650, subject to the 50% of W-2 wages rule.

Using the Section 861 Method we would go back and look at each print job and calculate the combined DPGR, COGS, and allocable indirect costs. In theory, this method should give us a result very similar to the SDM, but the requirement to capitalize costs may shift the numbers a bit.

The point here is that the easiest method isn't always the biggest deduction. A good accounting system is the best way to ensure that the deduction is maximized. The taxpayer must also have a reasonable basis for his accounting system and allocations of DPGR, COGS, and indirect costs and be consistent in its application.

DPAD Is Not an Election

One of the great aspects of DPAD is that it is not considered an election, meaning that if you fail to take the deduction, you can still go back and claim it within the three-year statute of limitations for filing an amended return. It is also important to note that although we call it an allocation "method," it is not considered an "accounting method" that requires IRS approval to change. The fact that DPAD is not an election means that once an allocation method is chosen it can still be changed from year to year. Thus, if you took the SOM this year, you can take the SDM next year. You could even change the method on an amended return if it made a significant difference. This means that there is a lot of flexibility for those who take advantage of this great deduction.

There Are Some Limitations

The DPAD is not recognized by all states, so although the IRS allows the adjustment to income for federal purposes, it may not be allowed under state law.

DPAD may only be taken by one taxpayer in the process and is generally the one that originally manufactured, produced, grew, or extracted the Qualified Production Property in the US, and/or had the benefits and burdens of ownership during the process. It is important for the taxpayer to clarify, in any contracts with suppliers or contractors, who is entitled to take the deduction and with respect to all aspects of the production process.

Taking the deduction requires that production be completed in "whole or in significant part within the US." The IRS has a safe harbor interpretation that roughly translates into a 20% threshold of the direct labor and overhead costs being incurred in the US.

Gross receipts from warranties, delivery, operating manuals, installation, or service agreements are not considered DPGR when these charges are separately-stated or sold independently. When revenue from these activities is 5% or less of the total gross receipts, they are considered *de minimis* and are included in DPGR.

Real-Life Examples

The Electrical Contractor

A local electrical contractor was referred to me by his investment advisor. He was concerned because after paying estimated taxes each quarter he had nothing left to fund their Simplified Employee Pension. The business pre-wires new homes, installs standby power systems, provides service contracts, and performs general repair services. One of the strategies we used to lower taxes was DPAD. DPAD saved the client about $5,000 a year in tax, and in conjunction with the strategies we used we were able to lower his adjusted gross income from $220,000 to just under $160,000, making him eligible to claim the American Opportunity Tax Credit for his two college-age children. We also went back and amended returns for the three prior years allowed and reclaimed DPAD. All told, we saved the client about $62,000 in the first year.

The HVAC Contractor

An HVAC contractor contacted our firm about tax planning. We reviewed his business model to see if he would qualify for DPAD and found that he did not. Although the company was installing equipment that would otherwise qualify for the credit, it was ineligible because its customers bought the equipment elsewhere—the company was install-only. We suggested that he restructure his transactions and actually buy the HVAC equipment, then sell it to the customer as part of the capital-improvement project. Once he had the benefits and burden of the inventory being used, he qualified. He found that buying the equipment himself allowed him to negotiate a lower price from the vendor and get a markup on the materials sold. Customers saved on the sales tax. The contractor's revenue doubled, profitability increased by about 25%, and he was able to cut his tax bill by about 10%.

The Farmer

A family-run farm sells a variety of farm products, including trees, seasonal fruits and vegetables, hay, and sheerings from sheep and alpaca. The owner was aware of DPAD, but knew he didn't qualify because he didn't have any employees. When we asked the farmer why he didn't put his wife and five kids on the payroll, he said he didn't want to pay $600 per year to the payroll company. We explained that putting his kids on payroll would cut his personal taxes by 50 cents for every dollar paid in wages. We also showed him how the wages paid to his two adult children would qualify him for DPAD. Our recommendations yielded about $40,000 in tax savings.

The Computer Company

I offered a free mini tax-planning session to my computer vendor several times over a couple of years. He always told me he liked to do his own taxes using a popular off-the-shelf tax software. When he finally met with me, we discovered he was not claiming DPAD on his income from custom-building computer systems. Furthermore, we discovered that off-the-shelf software either didn't handle the deduction or didn't prompt the taxpayer to claim it. When we reviewed the deduction, we calculated that he was entitled to a deduction of about $22,500 in the current year, which equated to a savings of about $5,625. When we went back and amended three years of returns, we found over $20,000 in savings related to DPAD.

The Real-Estate Developer

A real-estate developer purchased 30 acres of land and built 10 homes. The cost of the project included the costs to subdivide, excavate, build roads, and build the houses. All of the houses were substantially similar. Tax rules require that the costs of the project be capitalized. As each home sold, the selling price represented the DPGR, and the allocated costs, determined by the Section 861 Method, determined the QPAI, which multiplied by 9% equals the deduction. The deduction for each year is based on an item-by-item basis, whereby the calculation of the sale of each house is done separately taking into account the sales price, capitalized costs of goods sold, and any indirect costs associated with the sale. Interestingly, as the price of the unsold homes increases, so does the potential deduction, which going forward can help offset costs and any depreciation recapture.

Don't Try to Be Your Own Private Eye

If you have gotten this far, you have learned that DPAD is a great deduction for small businesses that qualify. I have illustrated this chapter in terms as easy as possible. Although the actual math involved in the calculation of the deduction is quite simple, it is important to recognize that the rules for applying this deduction may be complicated and may best be left to a qualified professional.

DPAD is a very complicated section of the tax code because it hasn't been thoroughly defined by the IRS and is just beginning to be tested in court. IRS policy points to a broad interpretation of the application of DPAD, but at the same time the IRS recognizes the need for heavy scrutiny to deter fraud.

Maintaining an accurate accounting system is essential to maximizing the Section 199 deduction. It is very important to develop a consistent basis for separating qualifying receipts from those that are not. Understanding and properly accounting for the direct and indirect expenses associated with this deduction are also important. Separating indirect costs is likely to increase the deduction but requires an item-by-item cost accounting method. Restructuring transactions to include purchasing materials to meet the "Benefits and Burdens of Ownership" test and evaluating the use of W-2 employees instead of subcontracting work also require continual review to meet the strict guidelines. Many clients find that retaining their Certified Tax Coach under an annual service contract is the most efficient way to maximize the deduction and meet the requirements of the law.

Let's Review Our Clues:

- Small-business owners must manage tax liability to compete in the global marketplace while maintaining profitability.
- The Domestic Production Activities Deduction (DPAD) is a little-known yet highly valuable deduction for goods that are manufactured, produced, grown, or extracted in the United States while promoting employment.
- The DPAD applies to many farming activities and may apply to fishing and to mining for minerals and other natural re-sources. Qualified films or TV productions, electricity, natural gas, or potable water produced in the US qualify. DPAD also includes construction, engineering, and

architectural services performed in the US for construction projects in the US.

- The requirement of paying wages is the deciding factor in claiming DPAD.

- The range of businesses that qualify for DPAD is much wider than most people think.

- Calculating the deduction for DPAD can be done with three methods: the Small Business Simplified Overall Method (SOM), the Simplified Deduction Method (SDM), or the Section 861 Method. They most often yield different deduction amounts, so you will want to use the method that works best for your business.

- You reclaim DPAD within the three-year statute of limitations for filing an amended return.

- DPAD is not recognized by all states, so although the IRS allows the adjustment to income for federal purposes it may not be allowed under state law.

- Finding a Certified Tax Coach that understands the rules of this Section 199 deduction can generate significant tax savings for you without creating additional expenses.

Be a savvy sleuth and take your case to the pros to see if you can take advantage of the DPAD.

Endnotes

1   U.S. v. Dean, et al (112 AFTR 2d 2013-5592)

2   FAA 20133302F

3   Gibson & Associates, Inc. 136 TC No.10

4   Reg. 1.199-3(i)(6)(iii)(B); CCA 201226025

5   Reg. 1-199-3(j)(1)

6   Rev Proc 2002-28; Reg. 1.199-4(f)

7   Reg. 1.99-4(e)

ABOUT THE AUTHOR

Pat O'Hara, EA, CTC

I solve tax problems! As a Certified Tax Coach, I help small-business owners pay less tax and have more money available to reinvest in their businesses, find money to save for retirement, or just have more money to do the things they want to do.

I work with building contractors, farmers, winemakers, caterers, small manufacturers, and craftsman in New York's Hudson Valley, and show them how to take advantage of tax incentives that most tax professionals miss or don't understand how to apply. One of the most missed deductions for these types of business owners is the subject of my chapter.

Too many clients come to me because they are in trouble with the IRS or state tax authorities. As an Enrolled Agent and Fellow of the National Tax Practice Institute, I have a reputation for resolving tax controversy. Most small businesses get into tax trouble because they don't plan to pay less tax and don't know how to take advantage of favorable provisions in the tax code. I became a Certified Tax Coach to help my clients reduce their tax burden before problems arise.

In 24 years helping people solve tax problems, I have seen more workers become small-business owners. Many of these business owners are stunned to find they end up paying 50% or more in tax on their hard-earned income. I develop tax-saving strategies that best utilize deductions, credits, and loopholes to prevent this from happening. Many of my clients find tax savings of $10,000 or more in the first year. My clients have realized that good tax planning is life changing and sets them onto the path to greater profitability and financial security.

Unlike many tax professionals, I take the time to learn about my clients' businesses and see firsthand how they earn their income. I enjoy touring their facilities and learning their work processes. I review their prior-year returns and put together a comprehensive tax plan with multiple strategies to reduce their income taxes and mitigate the risk of audit. I also help my clients choose the best strategies to implement, so they see an immediate return on their tax-planning investment.

If you would like to learn more, look for me on LinkedIn or Google at "Tax Alternative Group, LLC." You are also welcome to sign up for my free weekly Personal Strategy Notes at patrickohara.mylocaltaxpro. com.

My office number is (845) 242-2151, and my web address is Tax-AlternativeGroup.Com.

"Observation is your greatest tool, perception is your validation, investigation is your confirmation, Truth is your goal and freedom."

CHAPTER 14

The Unbreakable Alibi

Understanding Audit Risk Without Fearing the IRS

Francesco Arlia Jr., CPA, CGMA, CTC

We talk a lot in this book about being tax detectives to make good tax planning choices and also resolve problems. In this chapter, we are *literally* talking about tax investigations! It's time to get ready to not just be a sleuth, but to know what to do to avoid the inspection of *your* taxes, and how to proceed if an audit does indeed take place.

When it comes to income taxes, perhaps the biggest mystery of all: why are some people audited when others are not? It's certainly a mystery that needs to be solved if you want to avoid an audit of your own income taxes. Once you understand how an audit can be triggered, you can take steps to avoid those circumstances. You'll also be in a better position to defend your choices if you do find yourself being called for an audit. Let's delve deeply into this mystery to uncover the nine biggest clues that will tip-off the IRS that you are a candidate for an audit.

Before investigating those clues, let's first understand some history. The IRS has been auditing and seeking out tax cheats since its permanent inception in 1913. The actual beginnings of an income tax system derived out of necessity. The origins of the IRS started with the American Civil War (1861-65). Required funds to cover war expenses forced President Lincoln and Congress to propose a federal income tax and pass the Revenue Act of 1862. The act also established a federal agency, the Bureau of Internal Revenue, and the senior office of the Commissioner of Internal Revenue, to oversee tax collection.

Ten years later (Circa 1872) the income tax was repealed. Although Congress attempted to reinstate an income tax in 1894, the Supreme Court ruled it unconstitutional a year later. Income taxes had then been proposed and permanent in 1913 under then President Woodrow Wilson in his first year in office, when the Sixteenth Amendment to the Constitution was ratified, authorizing Congress to enact an income tax.

In 1953 the bureau was renamed the Internal Revenue Service. Just for kicks president Woodrow Wilson also proposed and passed The Federal Reserve Act that created the Federal Reserve and I need not say anything else. (Article Source: http://EzineArticles.com/1346488)

Up until 1997, the IRS conducted its audits by random selection computer processes that had little to no logic in choosing audit target groups or selectees.

The other method used was informants.

You would be surprised to find o ut t hat t here a re m any f ormer spouses and former employees who report questionable tax practices and thus become informants for the IRS. In fact, today there is even a reward program for informants: "THE WHISTLEBLOWER PROGRAM".

The IRS Whistleblower Office pays money to people who blow the whistle on persons who fail to pay the tax that they owe. If the IRS uses information provided by the whistleblower, it can award the whistleblower up to 30 percent of the additional tax, penalty and other amounts it collects.

Setting aside the informant route, the IRS truly had a failing audit selection system until fully revised by Mr. Charles Rissotti from 1997 –2002. Mr. Rossotti was appointed by then President Bill Clinton. IRS' Restructuring and Reform Act prompted the most comprehensive reorganization and modernization of IRS in nearly half a century. Today, computer technology produces algorithms that enable software to se-lect better targets, making the audit process more efficient and profit-able for the IRS. You can imagine that, with the advancements of the internet, information age, and advanced computer programming, the IRS is getting more aggressive in finding and targeting good selectees.

What is an Audit, Anyway?

Simply put, an audit is an investigation initiated by the IRS to en-sure that a person or company's income, deductions, and credits are being reported accurately to arrive at the correct tax liability. In gen-eral, audits happen when the IRS suspects a taxpayer is underreport-ing income, over-reporting deductions, or otherwise not paying their fair share in taxes. Our firm specializes in representing and defend-ing clients during an audit. You may be surprised to learn that the outcome of many of our cases is that our client actually overpaid the government over a period of years prior to the audit; we often find so many errors from prior accountants that the corrections outweigh the reported liability and actually result in additional refunds. As you can see, you don't always need to be afraid of an audit, but you do want to make sure you have a great team with a proven track record to defend you.

Audits can happen through the mail or in person. The tax auditor might come to your home, place of business, office of your accountant, or any other representative to conduct the invest-igation, or you might need to meet with him at a tax office. Regardless of the type of audit, you'll be notified of it through mail or a phone call. (Phone calls are very rare and you should be aware of the existence of scammers who call and impersonate the IRS).The communication will be to tell you what documents to bring to complete the investigation.

An audit doesn't always result in charges or penalties. If you're careful about following the law, you don't have anything to fear from an audit. However, they can be time-consuming and stressful, and auditors can easily bully people into paying more taxes than they actually owe simply because the taxpayer doesn't know any better. This is why it's so important to have a tax professional on your side who can protect you in the event that your business is audited. The best defense is a good offense, though, so knowing the strategies to audit-proof your business will save you a lot of hassles and can keep your risk of being audited low.

How the IRS Chooses Who to Audit

The IRS simply does not have the staff to individually comb through each tax return and audit anyone who looks suspicious. Instead, it uses a number of screening methods, most of them computerized, in order to sift through returns and find those that might be inaccurate. When this is done, those audits that have the most potential profitability from tax penalties are prioritized. If you know about the clues that can trigger an audit, you'll know how to avoid the trouble that comes along with one. In today's environment of advanced computer technology, the IRS uses the following systems:

Triggers – These could be indicated by a drop in normal trends from industry standards from prior reporting or from specific algorithms created by IRS intelligence. To keep it simple, a trigger is something that doesn't make sense and is questionable. Not all triggers will bring about an audit.

Mismatching – This is caused by incorrect or inconsistent reporting of a taxpayer or his accountant as compared to the reporting of a third party. A simple example is if you reported for services on your schedule "C" as a self-employed individual and the parties you serviced reported 1099's that exceeded what you reported. This will immediately trigger a letter; if the difference is high enough and the remainder of the tax return is questionable, it may very well trigger an audit. The IRS has been increasing reporting requirements to ensure that third party information matches tax returns, increasing the potential for the discovery of a mismatch and a new audit target.

Informants – This program has always existed but now it is coupled with incentives and a BONUS. The IRS website each year updates the "Whistleblower Program" and informs the public accordingly.

Special Selection – This unit deals with everything from Form 8300 reports (cash transactions of $10,000 or greater or suspicious transac-tions). For example, imagine that someone goes to the bank to deposit $4000 and the money smells like marijuana. The teller can file a report of a suspicious transaction to the IRS. Other special selection comes from the court system when an individual is arrested and convicted of an illegal act that had financial benefits associated with it and that may or may not have been reported. Remember that, even though a crime resulted in a conviction on the civil level, it could have been perfectly legal in tax court. There are many other special selection processes, but they make up for a minority of audit cases.

Tax Returns That Don't Match Other Reports

Whenever you fill out a W-2 or other type of tax document using your SSN or TIN, that document gets forwarded to the IRS. If the documents that get sent in have information that disagrees with what you send in with your own tax return, a mismatch occurs and normally precipitates a standard letter questioning the accuracy. If your tax return has other triggers, you will be audited.

Note that you may not know whether your employer has incorrect information until after you receive a 1099. By the time you receive one, the IRS will already have a copy. You can avoid an audit in a case like this with some standard due diligence. Most employers these days know they need to gather correct information from employees and vendors or sub-contractors. If you're not asked for information before starting consulting work, then you should offer the information and be proactive about the reporting. If you are still unable to avoid a discrepancy and you cannot fix it in time, a good tax professional will be able to address the situation with the IRS. A tax coach can coordinate the legwork involved in making sure that the documents are amended and match up.

Ignoring an Inquiry Letter

If you get a document in the mail from the IRS, it's always in your best interest to respond to it swiftly. These inquiries are considered pre-audits; they give you the chance to explain yourself before a full investigation is launched. Avoiding the letter or delaying your response doesn't make you look good, and it will invite further investigation.

Of course, it's always possible that you didn't realize that the letter was sent in the first place. If your address is out of date, you might be missing tax correspondence. This can be a problem since the IRS communicates about audits through the mail; if you miss an appointment because you didn't know you were supposed to be there for it, you can get yourself into more trouble. Always be sure that the information you have on file is accurate, and smooth over any problems with the post office before tax season rolls around. The IRS and state tax boards both have specific (usually one page and simple) forms that can be downloaded and filled out to advise the agencies of your new mailing address and other important information, and some states have downloadable forms online. We have represented several cases wherein the taxpayer relocated and was not on notice that the audit was initiated, and it was addressed and closed without the taxpayer involved. Protocol exists to correct such situations, but you can imagine all the additional work required and related costs. A mistake like this can easily double the standard costs of an audit.

Claiming Reimbursable Employee Expenses

Here's a big one that can trip you up: if you work for a company and take business expense deductions, you can find yourself in trouble with the IRS. This is because many companies are supposed to reimburse their employees for business expenses, and they claim those reimbursements on their own tax returns. The IRS keeps a list of the major companies that are supposed to be reimbursing their workers, and if your employer is on that list, you can get audited for your expense deductions. This is now a trigger from a special algorithm designed by the IRS that has been implemented for a few years now. Tax preparers must report every employer W-2 received and the W-2 specifics. There is very specific tax law that clearly states that if a company has a reimbursement policy and you choose not to take advantage of it, you also lose the deductibility option; the stance the government takes is that you should have taken advantage of the reimbursement policy. Know your company policy. If you're self-employed, you certainly want to speak to a smart tax coach to prepare and write company policy and employment contracts, as this can save you thousands if not millions of dollars (depending on the size of your company).

From the perspective of the IRS, it makes sense to investigate deductions for expenses that are reimbursable, since double-dipping or violation of specific reimbursement rules may be occurring. The problem is that you, as an employee, may not realize that your company was supposed to reimburse you in the first place. Obviously this would not be a defendable excuse for an employed individual; as an employee you should be well aware of company policy. If you are self-employed, the same reasoning applies, as you must be aware of your own policy. All the more reason to have your company policy and employment contracts written by a Certified Tax Coach and reviewed by an HR attorney.

Fortunately, a smart tax coach can help you counteract this problem in a few ways. We can find the differences between what is allowable by law and what is not under regulation. An example of a big gray area is gas reimbursement, since employers often reimburse gas at a lower rate than the IRS. In other cases, there may be some limitations on expense reimbursements written into the company's policies. Knowing the policies inside and out and combining this with a thorough knowledge of tax law can ensure that you can defend your deductions, or at least a portion of them. The real detective work in protecting taxpayers is finding what other accountants missed or what may have been missed during the tax return preparation interview.. It also comes from great communication and understanding of what the taxpayer does day-to-day. These are questions that not every tax professional asks but should. They are also questions that every taxpayer should want to answer in detail but don't. Tax professionals must be fully informed before advising on deductibles. The ability to gather the right data is another great tax detective trait.

Incorrectly Claimed Charitable Deductions

Donating to Charity or any approved tax-deductible organization is honorable just for the act of supporting others. The IRS regulations make some charitable deductions more complicated and loaded with red tape. The truth of the matter is that regulations are put in place because of the few who take advantage of the deduction and overstate charitable donations. They have created an environment that is an over regulated, over scrutinized, and highly reviewed area of tax deductions. If a charitable contribution is large, it will be thoroughly scrutinized by the IRS, and an innocent mistake in reporting by either the recipient party or the donating party could create a noticeable mismatch. This could either trigger an audit or raise attention to review the remainder of the return for other discrepancies that can provide additional cause for an audit.

To claim a charitable deduction, you'll generally need to submit correctly filled out supporting forms in the case of non-cash transactions. If providing cash donations the reporting is not as complicated, however support is still required. If there's anything wrong with the submission documents, you may trigger an audit. This is frustrating for taxpayers because the errors on the forms are often a result of incorrect reporting of the charitable organization itself.

The unfortunate truth is that any charitable deduction over $250 can be denied during an audit unless you have the charity's acknowledgment letter on hand as support for each donation. This letter must state the amount of the donation, a description of any donated items, and a statement about whether any goods or services were exchanged for the donation. If any part of this information is inaccurate, the deduction can be turned down according to the IRS rules. However, most

IRS agents don't want to deny you the deduction. If you have proof of payment and a good assertive tax defense representative who understands how to apply alternative defense procedures such as "The Cohan Rule," you will be covered. The Cohan Rule comes from a federal court decision from 1930; it's legal citation is Cohan vs. Commissioner, 39F. 2d 540 (2d Cir. 1930). George Cohan was a famous producer in the theater industry whose statue stands proud and tall in the center of NYC Times Square. He was one of the first taxpayers to be audited. In his case, the Federal Appeals court ruled that he had allowable business expenses, even though they were undocumented approximations. The Cohan Rule, if applied properly, can help defend a case lacking necessary documentation. However, acceptance of the Cohan Rule of allowable approximate deductions is always discretionary with a court; a taxpayer is not automatically entitled to make approximations in tax matters and needs to provide foundational proof of expenses incurred. It never hurts to bring up the Cohan Rule in court as a means to argue for deductions for undocumented expenses for charitable contributions and beyond.

A High DIF Score

DIF, or the Discriminate Information Function, is the database that the IRS uses to filter out potentially inaccurate tax information. Basically, every return that's processed is compared against others from people with similar incomes, career types, family size, neighborhoods, and other demographic information. Variations from these averages raise your DIF, and a high DIF score will translate into a tax audit. This is also considered a trigger.

Of course, this can be very frustrating for the taxpayer as there may be a perfectly sound reason for being different from others in similar situations. You may have a larger family and claim more deductions for it than most people in your neighborhood. You may earn substantially more or less than other people in your field, especially if you're self-employed. You may receive financial assistance that doesn't count as income, like gifts from your parents or child support from an ex-spouse, causing a mismatch between your lifestyle and reportable income. Since the DIF system is automated, the IRS won't notice or care: even if everything else in your tax return is in order, a high DIF can still trigger an investigation. I use the word investigation, as a high DIF score will usually trigger further review of the return. The IRS sys-tem also performs a Cost Benefit Analysis to determine if good tax-payer dollars should be spent for possiblly bad tax collection results. A high DIF score may not always trigger an audit but it will surely put you in the spotlight.

Reporting Too Little Income

One of the most frustrating ways a DIF score can affect you is if you seem to be making too little money. The IRS will look at your oc-cupation, deductions, family size, and where you live and determine how much money you should need in order to live in that area. If that amount comes up as higher than your income, you'll be earmarked for an audit even if there is nothing wrong with your tax return. The same rules will always apply with respect to other discrepancies that can trigger an audit. Remember, we are working toward the reduction of audit risk. In others words, we want to eliminate or reduce triggers and mismatching as much as possible.

The policy of comparing your cost of living to your income was put in place primarily to catch self-employed individuals who underreport their incomes, but it fails to take into account mitigating factors like frugality and financial help from family members. If the IRS thinks you can't live on the income that is expected for your circumstances, you could be assumed to be underreporting and be audited.. The other part of this equation is just pure logic. If your self-employed income is so low that it is below economic standards for your demographic area, then why not logically seek other employment? The IRS can even demand a cost of living audit, wherein you answer very specific sur-vey questions to determine your true cost of living... The IRS would then compare that data with your income, and even verify the income and expenses against deposits and payments or withdrawals from your personal bank accounts and usage of your credit cards and credit lines. Be aware that very smart tax professionals know how to use these same rules in your defense when the case calls for such actions.

Using Round Numbers

This is the easiest and most foolish way to trigger an audit. Any tax professional that files or allows the taxpayer to use round numbers should be fired immediately. This is logical thinking-101. They don't teach this stuff in college, you either know it or you will learn the hard way. When you claim deductions, you have to give exact figures. If the IRS suspects that you're rounding, it will invite an audit. Today computers are so much more easily programmed and algorithms so easily created that rounding is a trigger; careful review of other possi-ble discrepancies is used just to determine the cost-benefit calculation of conducting the audit. In simpler terms, the IRS is smarter and more efficient, and you can't afford to make avoidable mistakes or use careless logic. Whether you're reporting your income or making a deduction, a round number like 100 or 1200 will invite suspicion. Keep your return as accurate as possible by using exact figures down to the dollars and rounded to cents only, and be sure you have receipts to back up every claim you make. It may sound difficult but is really easy to stay organized once you make the decision to use a good system and get underway.

Income From Cancellation of Debt

This is a clue that many people don't know about, and it can get you into trouble if you're not careful. If you have a debt that has been forgiven for any reason, you can be taxed on the amount that you would have otherwise owed. In other words, the forgiven debt gets treated as income and is taxed accordingly. This can apply to any sort of debt, including real estate, and it can come as a shock to an unsuspecting taxpayer. Those who technically received a financial benefit via loans, credit card advances, or purchases, but never actually had to pay the monies back to the lending institution, are viewed upon as receiving a taxable financial benefit, hence a taxable event if the debt is reported as canceled. This is where the mismatch occurs that leads to the trigger that then leads to the audit. In many cases the original reporting documents are sent to an old address on file or the last known address, therefore the taxpayer never actually received it in the first place. This area of the tax code is complex and full of options, so you'll need a good tax professional to guide you through. In many cases the cancellation of debt can actually be mitigated and or eliminated by understanding the intricacies of the IRS regulations.

Gambling Winnings and Losses Reporting

Unless you're a high roller in Vegas, you may not know that you can claim your gambling losses on your tax return. You also may not realize that you need to claim your gambling winnings. The catch is, in order to claim your losses they must only be offset by gains: you can't claim more in losses than the amount you won. Gain less loss equals difference. Also, as any lottery-winner knows, your gambling income is taxed as regular income. The gain is reported on page one of form 1040 and the loss is reported on Schedule A (Itemized Deductions). The most horrible situation one could be in is when the losses and other itemized deductions are not great enough to actually qualify to file Schedule A, and therefore you can't offset the losses against the gain.

If you did win some money this year, you should absolutely offset the cost of your gambling income tax by claiming your losses. In order to make this strategy work, however, you'll need the appropriate paperwork to back up your claim. Be prepared to show every ticket, receipt or statement that you have detailing both wins and losses, especially if you are gambling at an organization that is not well organized. Without the appropriate paperwork, all of your deductions will be rejected. Then again, the info can be easy to track with computer technology and customer service management at an organized facility; you can just call your casino and ask that a win loss statement be prepared in a matter of minutes. The IRS already knows that most people lose; if they didn't, casinos wouldn't be incredibly extravagant and constantly expanding. Just be prepared to show those losses. There is no fun in paying taxes on gambling winnings that could have been offset with losses. It's like losing twice on the same bet.

Don't Go In Unprepared or Unrepresented

Now that we've seen nine basic clues that the IRS will look at to determine whether your account is worthy of an audit, we've gone a long way toward solving the mystery of why some people get audited. For the most part, people are audited because there are triggers, mismatching, informants, and special selection. The majority of audits come from triggers and mismatching evident on the tax return. These problems can be avoided by making sure you are filing your tax return with a proven professional with a good reputation and intricate understanding of your business. You can easily do independent searches on the internet and find plenty of information about whom you are considering to hire, prepare, and file your annual tax return.

Knowing the problems that can easily arise when not using a competent tax professional, you should always rely on the help of a savvy tax planner that can maximize your tax savings while also minimizing your audit risk. It will also helps to have someone on your side with a proven track record of defending cases, as that is the first hint that he or she knows the regulations and laws and can defend your return if necessary. After all, trying to represent yourself during an audit is about as effective as writing out a blank check to the IRS. Your best defense in saving money, reducing audit risk, and being covered if an audit does arise is your organization, maintenance of records and partnership with a stellar tax coach. When choosing a professional always look for these clues of a highly effective tax coach:

1. Is the office organized? If it's not then you are already in the wrong place. The errors are just waiting to happen.

2. Is the place clean? A true professional cares as much about his own work environment as he cares about his work.

3. How is his communication? Does he listen? Does he ask several valid questions? Is he encouraging your consideration of applicable deductions?

4. Is he courteous and customer service oriented? If not showing care for you and your family, how do you think he will treat your paperwork and filing obligation?

5. Does he have a proven track record of good service, including multiple testimonials available for your review?

6. Does he have a proven track record of defending cases against the IRS? Here's a case study of two clients of mine, two real estate partners, both of them full time mortgage brokers working for commercial banks. One partner, whom we will call Mr. S., had a tax return that had many fluctuations and trigger points but the deductions and income were correct and per my professional opinion he qualified as a real estate professional. The second partner, whom we will call Mr. L., also qualified as a real estate professional by my standards and interpretation of the law. Mr. S. was audited and first he attempted to handle it on his own against my professional advice. Eventually he asked me to quote the cost of the defense case, which was $4500 at that time. He decided to hire another tax advisor at a much lower cost, and the end result was a failed case, rejected real estate professional status, tax fees, penalties, interest, etc. Mr. L was later advised by his partner (Mr. S.) that he would be audited and encounter the same problems. I assured Mr. L, who continues to be my client, that this would not be the case. Nine months later the audit arrived. We gathered our documents, defended the case, won on all levels including his real estate tax professional designation, and also discovered additional deductions with information that had not been shared by Mr. S. We ended up with an additional refund at the end of the audit! Any tax professional will tell you that the case I defended was seemingly impossible to win considering the circumstances, but I know my regulations and I know how to defend cases. I deliver results. In 24 years I have defended

over 74 major cases with 74 knockouts and 0 losses. That is a track record I am very proud of.

The IRS Wants Your Money

The IRS would not go to the trouble of auditing taxpayers if it wasn't profitable. It takes time and effort to review an account, send a notice, and complete an audit. The IRS won't bother with this effort if there is no money to be had. In other words, when they meet with you, these auditors plan to leave the meeting with as much money as they can to make all of the effort worthwhile.

For the uninformed taxpayer, this can result in agreeing to pay things without fully understanding the implications. Here's a secret the IRS isn't eager to tell you: when you're audited for one year, those same penalties can be applied to the two other open years. Even more importantly, if you lose the fight on one year they will more than likely open the other two years with just cause. If the IRS audit does not yield profits, however, they lose the right to examine the two open years and cannot audit you on the same issues for the next three years. Also be advised that an IRS agent will usually ask you to provide prior year tax returns as a gesture that it is "standard procedure." However, if it is not part of the original IDR (Information Document Request) then it is a seemingly friendly ploy to open up prior years covertly. This is a clear indication that you need to immediately hire a legitimate professional with proven track record.

Imagine this situation: you're audited because you earn $30,000 as a freelancer, but, based on the income of others in your neighborhood with the same family size, the IRS believes that you must be making at least $40,000. Of course, the IRS isn't taking into account that you've been living frugally and had some assistance from child support payments and a few small gifts from your family, so they start sending you letters about money that you owe. At this point, it's not uncommon to feel a sense of panic or shame, even though you did nothing wrong. You might go ahead and agree to pay the money simply because the IRS says that you're supposed to. As soon as you agree to it, though, the IRS takes this as an admission of guilt and might conclude that you must have been unethical on other tax returns as well. You can end up being charged for three years of under-reported income, with a tax bill that's much higher than what you had anticipated. Worse yet, the IRS can charge you an accuracy penalty on top of this to make your tax bill even higher, with related interest that can be compounded if you don't fight for simple interest.

This is just one example of what could happen if you admit guilt, surrender your rights, and/or lose a case. Most cases should be fought to a final result. My longest case was fought for five years. It started out as a $125,000 liability demand from the IRS, and after five long years resulted in a $3,000 refund and $12,000 carryover passive loss. It has been 18 years since and my client has never been audited again. Tax defense is a sophisticated area of expertise that should only be undertaken with excellent representation.

A Smart Financial Advisor is the Best Defense You Can have

This situation may seem surreal, but it's the reality more often than you'd like to believe. In my time as a Certified Public Accountant and Certified Tax Coach, I'd estimate that as many as 85% of the IRS notices sent to my clients have been false or inaccurate. Sadly, many people just don't realize that you can dispute these notices, inquiries, and audits, and they end up paying a lot more than they really owe just because the IRS's computer system decided the taxpayer must have filing errors.

As a tax detective, you know better than to take this lying down. The IRS has tactics for getting the most money from you; you need to fight back with smart tax strategies that keep you from paying more money than you owe. This book helps arm you with the knowledge to reduce your tax bill without incurring any unnecessary audits; having a tax professional in your corner will seal the deal. To win all of my cases, I put on my Sherlock Holmes detective hat and went directly into forensic accounting mode to delve into the details missed by the prior accountant. Then I would offset any mistakes discovered by the IRS with mistakes from the prior accountant that were in my client's favor. This ended up with minimum break-even results but more often a refund for my client. My firm is always up to a challenge of detecting accounting errors on all levels and helping our clients financially in a very significant way.

Let's Review Our Clues

One of the biggest mysteries in tax law is why some people are audited while others never catch attention of the IRS. Let's look back at the clues we've uncovered about why that happens:

- The IRS uses automated systems and algorithms to detect and review tax returns, and those automated systems are not always accurate.

- The IRS uses triggers, mismatching, informants, and special selection procedures to procure audit prospects.

- Some things that can trigger an audit are out of your control, like an employer or charity filling out tax forms incorrectly. You can mitigate this damage by spotting the errors early and requesting that an amended version be sent to the IRS. This is mismatching.

- Failing to respond to correspondence from the IRS can escalate the situation; always be sure you have an accurate address on file.

- Your DIF score is one of the primary ways the IRS identifies tax returns to flag for an audit provided that some other triggers exist and the audit looks to be a good financial investment for them. The DIF selection process alone won't initiate an audit.

- If your income deviates from what the IRS expects for a person in your situation, you can be flagged for an investigation that can lead to other triggers and then an audit even if there's nothing wrong with your return.

- Always avoid round numbers and use accurate numbers. Be careful with major triggers, such as charitable contributions, cancellation of debt, gambling transactions, and excessive employee deductions.

- The IRS will always opt for an audit if it believes that it can make money. You won't be audited for overpaying your taxes, but you will be audited if the IRS thinks you're not paying your share. Simply stated, if the IRS believes it is 100% correct and the financial benefits are high enough, rather than send a notice, you will receive an audit investigation letter with an attached IDR (Information Document Request) form.

- Tax laws are not always fair or easy to understand, and the IRS takes advantage of that fact in order to get you to pay more than you owe. It's your job to fight back with a smart tax strategy. A smart tax strategy always includes a savvy tax professional, such as a Certified Tax Coach.

ABOUT THE AUTHOR

Francesco Arlia Jr., CPA, CGMA, CTC

Francesco Arlia Jr. is the managing partner of Arlia & Associates with offices in
Manhattan, Staten Island, and Clearwater,
Florida. His firm specializes in real estate
accounting, CFO outsourcing services,
start-up ventures, business engineering,
tax planning with a special focus on
"Unique Tax Strategies", and Internal
Revenue Defense Cases. His firm also
administers extensive business coaching

with clients, implementing management systems, automating
systems, improving hiring procedures, training and retaining key
personnel.

Arlia & Associates also networks and coordinates with several senior consultants and consulting firms both national and international
to avail all existing and new clients to both national and international
markets and services.

A graduate of Bernard M Baruch College, Mr. Arlia started his
career as an accountant after being informed by one of his most re-
spected college professors "As an accountant you have the opportunity
to defend the taxpayers against the government" That objective of defending the little guy, got me hooked. I am a fighter and in 25 years of
practicing, I have never lost a case. To date: 74 knockouts and 0 losses."

While pursuing his accounting degree, Mr. Arlia worked full-time
with the law and accounting firm of Marks, Macchiarolla & Savino
where he worked on local, national, and international projects for the
firm. With the help of Mr. Macchiarola he opened his own firm ARCO
Financial Services during his junior year of college. After graduation,
he continued working at both firms and added a third career as con-
troller for an auto dealership. By 1997, his own firm had grown to the
point where it required his full-time attention.

By 1999 he became a licensed CPA and pursued expanding his knowledge in real estate consulting via his extensive experience in real estate investing and real estate tax planning. He then continued to expand his firm with developing unique tax planning strategies for the middle class, once known to be only for the ultra rich.

By 2004 with the help of Sterling Management he started learning and implementing the Hubbard College of Administration & Management business technology and immediately discovered proven management technology that was simple and worked 100% of the time. "Within 16 months of applying the technology I doubled my firm and then began applying the technology to my client's business with extensive positive results." Applying these business practices has helped the accounting firm gain the "Know How" of running businesses from a CEO & CFO viewpoint to the degree that companies both national and international are entrusting Arlia & Associates with their administration and management from full accounting services to full operations.

"Although I am busier than ever and significantly more financially secure, I am not stressed out or working long hours. I am able to get more done in less time, I can take several months off each year, and I love helping my clients achieve similar results in their own businesses."

When asked what are my greatest strengths, the answer is simple. I pride myself on three main attributes and I teach these points to my ever growing family, friendships, and staff on a daily basis.

1) Being able to confront anything and handle accordingly.

2) Always look and find what others fail to see because there is always a solution to a problem and therefore solutions are your target.

3) Work hard, live life positively, and play harder because life is a game of cycles, the more you complete, the greater your success.

In addition to running a successful accounting firm that is also growing nationally, I am the proud father of three wonderful children. Alexsandra, Francesco III, and Sophia. I am active in my local community with literacy programs and anti-drug programs.

I am extensively active in fundraising monies for non-profit community betterment organizations, and have two CYO basketball championships under his belt as a youth inspirational coach.

On a personal note I enjoy life in the fast lanes as I train to race NASCARs. I aspire to soon be an amateur level race car driver winning championships on behalf of my favorite charities and community betterment organizations.

10 Jefferson Boulevard
Staten Island NY 10312

(718) 227-6864

www.aaacpallp.com

CHAPTER 15

Even Wacky Things
Can Reduce Your Taxes

By Robert (Bob) Korljan, CPA/PFS, AEP, CTC

Now that you've examined many clues about how to save money through proactive tax planning and smart financial strategies, it's time to put your knowledge to the test. We've talked a lot in this book about being a tax detective. Now, let's see if you can apply your detective skills to a few real-world examples.

First, we'll look at a few general tips for claiming successful deductions for unexpected items. After that, I'll show you some real examples of deductions that people have tried to make. See if you can put your detective skills to work and find out which of these cases worked, and which didn't.

Solving the Mystery of Great Tax Savings

So far, we've seen many specific tax strategies that can be applied to various situations. The challenge of tax planning is that there is no single viable strategy for squeezing value from deductions. A strategy that works for one business won't work for another, and you may not benefit from the same deductions as your neighbor or hair stylist.

Simply knowing that people have successfully made some off-the-wall tax deductions won't help you much unless you happen to be in exactly the same situation. Even subtle factors can make the difference between a successful tax strategy and one that fails. For example, there's a solid precedence in place for women in the adult entertainment business claiming breast augmentation surgery as a business expense. You'd be hard-pressed to claim that same deduction as a dance instructor.

In general, the goal of tax planning should always be to make the most of what you have. When it comes to deductions, this means finding ways to deduct your current expenses. In most cases, a creative accountant will find a way to deduct any major, ongoing, or meaningful expenses you incur for your business.

Documentation Makes All the Difference

Nearly any business expense can be deducted if it follows certain criteria:

- The expense is necessary and reasonably common for the type of work you do. For example, a video game reviewer can likely deduct the cost of games and gaming consoles. A real estate agent probably cannot.

- You can prove that an expense is reasonable and justified. This generally comes down to good bookkeeping.

- It meets the criteria for certain special deductions, such as making a business more eco-friendly or accessible to people with disabilities.

There's a lot of leeway in these rules for creative accounting. In every case of successful tax planning, the key is proper documentation. Good record-keeping is crucial to proving the business necessity of an item or activity, so that you can make a case for the deduction.

For example, imagine that you decide to take up beekeeping as a hobby. You sell some honey at the local farmers' market and make a small profit. If you could document a profit motive for the activity and maintain good records of your expenses and profits, you would be able to deduct things like the cost of bees, the hive, and specialized equipment, and these deductions could be used to offset your income from other sources. Without good records, though, your deductions may not be accepted, and you'll find yourself funding your beekeeping enterprise entirely out of your own pocket.

When it comes to tax planning, there's no such thing as too much documentation. You may not need everything that you keep, but it's always better to be over-prepared than caught off guard. Here are a few things you should get in the habit of documenting:

- The purpose of any item you purchase for your business.
- The exact cost of your necessary expenses. Remember that rounding can trigger an audit!
- The reason for any business travel, including where you went, why you were there, and who you connected with.
- Notes about business entertainment, including the exact cost, the purpose of the event, and your business relationship with the people you were meeting with or entertaining.

Much of this information should already have been kept in your appointment book, so a few extra notations are all you need to satisfy the IRS.

Other Deductible Expenses

Business owners are not the only people who can benefit from creative accounting. Although this book has been focused primarily on tax deductions for business expenses, there are plenty of other deductions that can be taken by anyone. The trick is to look at your personal expenses and discuss them with your accountant to see whether a case for a particular deduction might be made.

For example, many people are unaware that they can claim medical expenses on their taxes. If you have medical costs amounting to more than 10 percent of your total income, and these expenses are not reimbursed through your insurance or any other means, you can deduct them on your tax return. Be sure to check with your tax advisor, however, as there are exceptions that could reduce the percentage to as low as 7.5%. This is very valuable to people suffering from chronic illnesses that require a lot of medical care; it's also a smart tactic for years when you have a medical emergency.

These are not, however, the only opportunities for deducting medical expenses. You may find that certain unexpected costs can be deductible when they are prompted by a doctor's orders or medical necessity. For example, installation and maintenance of a hot tub might be deductible of it's used for physical therapy at your home. A gym membership could be deductible by an obese person whose doctor orders a weight loss program. In one notable case, a mother was even able to deduct the cost of clarinet lessons when they were recommended to treat her son's overbite!

Which of These Deductions Worked?

Now that we've investigated some of the underlying logic behind identifying tax opportunities, let's put our knowledge to the test. Here are six strange tax deductions that people actually tried to claim. Can you use your detective skills to determine which ones were actually accepted by the IRS?

1 – A woman began claiming her 20-year-old handyman as a dependent on her tax return, claiming that he was her nephew.

2 – A junkyard owner decided to deal with his pest infestation problem by attracting feral cats, claiming the costs of cat food as a business expense.

3 – A professional landscaper hired his dog as an employee by fixing him to a cart filled with tools in order to claim pet expenses.

4 – The owner of a wine shop made a medical expense claim for nasal surgery to improve his sense of smell.

5 – A woman with osteoarthritis claimed the cost of dance lessons as a medical expense after her doctor recommended it as therapy.

6 – A recent divorcee was able to claim 50% of her AGI as a deduction after donating all of her ex-husband's belongings.

Have you made your guesses? Let's see if you were right:

1 – This case, as you might have expected, was not accepted by the IRS. You can absolutely claim dependents on your tax return and will receive a deduction for each individual you claim. To keep this legal, however, your dependents need to be related to you. The deduction usually applies to children and stepchildren, but it can also apply to resident relatives in your care as long as they cannot be claimed by anyone else. This means that if your nephew lives with you after the death of his parents, you could claim him as a dependent, but you can't simply claim any young person who stays at your house.

2 – This one is actually legitimate. In fact, junkyard and farm owners are routinely able to deduct expenses related to guard dogs and vermin-hunting cats as these animals serve a clear business purpose. Barn cats are a common fixture at farms of all sizes as they help to keep the resident rodent population down. The arrangement described above is a little unorthodox since most people simply buy or adopt animals for this purpose, but with proper documentation the junkyard owner was able to state his case. If you're planning to try this yourself, just remember that the animal's purpose must be obvious and reasonable. Trying to claim a deduction for your pet dachshund under the pretense of "guard dog" may be a bit of a stretch.

3 – This clever idea didn't hold muster in the eyes of the IRS. While a guard dog can serve a business purpose, there's no clear reason why the landscaper would need a dog to pull a cart. Since cart-pulling dogs are not a common expense in the landscaping industry, there is no precedent for this type of deduction. Dogs,

even working dogs, also do not qualify as "employees" the way that people might. This landscaper would have been better off hiring his son to pull the cart and help with other light duties instead. Then he could have set aside money tax-free for his child's college fund and enjoyed some additional potential tax deductions for employee benefits.

4 – Surprisingly, this really did happen and was held up by the IRS. The accountant responsible drew on the precedent set by exotic dancers for breast augmentation surgery. In the case of the wine shop owner, an enhanced sense of smell was crucial to identifying the quality of the wines he sold, making this elective surgery a valid business expense.

5 – If you guessed that this deduction was legitimate, you were right. In this case, the key component was the doctor's orders: with written documentation that a doctor recommended dancing lessons, the woman and her accountant were able to legitimize $8,000 in dance-related expenses. It's worth noting that similar cases, like another woman who tried to claim dance-related expenses for her varicose veins, were denied due to lack of documentation. The woman from this example also attempted to claim several luxury cruises with her dance instructor, which were not permitted by the IRS.

6 – This, too, is a valid deduction, although the woman who made it missed a valuable opportunity. In this particular case, she actually donated $40,000 worth of items, including a very expensive set of golf clubs. Since $40,000 was higher than her income, she was unable to claim all of the expenses; the deduction was capped at 50% of her AGI. If she'd held onto some of the items, she could have donated them in subsequent years for additional tax deductions. Of course, if that were the case, her husband may have been able to take back his property. A smart tax strategy was most likely not the first thing on her mind when she dropped off his belongings at the local thrift

store. This example does illustrate, however, just how valuable clever accounting can be when it comes to making the most of your specific situation.

How did you do? If you got most of them right, you truly have become a tax detective! You know to look for important clues, like doctor's notes and business necessity. You also recognize when an expense is reasonable and common for a business.

Now, just for fun, let's examine a few more off-the-wall tax deductions that people have tried to make over the years.

Deductions for Illegal Activities

Drug dealers, prostitutes, and other shady businesspeople pay taxes just like everyone else. Most of the time, they do so through the front of more legitimate businesses, at least until they are caught. Nevertheless, the IRS is happy to take money from criminals. It will not give out tax deductions for illegal behaviors, however. Here are a few notable attempts people have made to write off their law-breaking expenses:

- An attorney racked up $64,000 in expenses with local prostitutes. His attempts to claim them as "medically necessary" didn't sway the IRS.

- Sometimes, desperate business owners will try to get out from under a failing business by destroying it and taking the insurance money. That was the case of a Pittsburgh man who hired an arsonist to burn down his building. He might have gotten away with this scheme if he had not tried to deduct the arsonist's fee on his tax return.

- Soil, lab equipment, grow lights, and other drug-related equipment cannot be deducted on your taxes unless, of course, you are licensed to legally grow marijuana in your state.

- As tempting as it may be, you can't deduct your parking tickets, even if you received them while attending an important business convention.

While illegal activities themselves are not deductible, there are a few surprising deductions you might be able to take if you ever find yourself on the wrong side of the law:

- The cost of checking into a drug rehab facility is tax deductible. On a more mundane note, smokers can also deduct the cost of smoking cessation aids like nicotine gum or patches.

- If you go to trial, you may be able to deduct the expense of hiring an attorney depending on the situation.

- If one of your employees is making shady business practices like over-charging customers, you may be able to claim the money you reimburse to those scam victims once the employee is caught.

Of course, your best bet is to always avoid illegal activities. If you don't incur any illegal expenses, you won't need to make any deductions for them.

Off-the-Wall Deductions That Totally Worked

We've already looked at some unexpected tax deductions, many of which are entirely legitimate in the eyes of the IRS. For fun, let's look at a few more examples that really illustrate the flexibility of tax laws:

- The precedent-setter for deductible breast augmentation surgery was Cynthia Hess, aka "Chesty Love." Since her bust size was a major part of this exotic dancer's act, she was able to claim the cosmetic surgery as a business expense.

- Musicians can deduct all sorts of clothing for stage performances. One member of Rod Stewart's band was able to deduct the cost of sparkly vests, outlandish hats, and leather pants. The IRS would not grant him a deduction for his flashy boxers, however.

- Professional bodybuilders can deduct all sorts of exhibition-related expenses, including posing oil and tanning lotion.

- Some particularly savvy businesspeople have learned to mix business and pleasure by shifting most of their business discussions to the golf course. This allows them to deduct the membership fees for the golfing club. A similar tactic could work well to fuel your Starbucks habit if you routinely meet your customers at the coffee shop.

The point of this chapter is not to give you a list of strange deductions to try claiming on your next tax return. The idea is simply to give you some inspiration about how flexible the tax code can be when you apply some creativity to it. When you look at your expenses, you may find many opportunities that you wouldn't expect. It definitely helps if there's a precedent in place for the type of deduction you're claiming, which is one area where having a savvy accountant can really help.

Let's Review Our Clues

- Tax law is surprisingly flexible.
- Many expenses can be deductible if the circumstances surrounding them are right.
- Deductions that are appropriate for one person or business may not work for another, so a personal tax-planning approach is always the most successful.
- Creative accounting runs the risk of inviting audits and fines only when it strays from the spirit of the tax code.
- Medical deductions are one area that many people forget to claim, but they can be a powerful tax reduction tool.
- Most business expenses can be claimed as long as they are common and reasonable for your business.
- Illegal activities are not deductible, but some surprising deductions can be made even by criminals.
- It's always best to have a savvy tax coach on your team before attempting any wacky tax deductions of your own.

ABOUT THE AUTHOR

Robert (Bob) Korljan, CPA/PFS, AEP, CTC

Robert has been helping small businesses and high-net-worth individuals with investment, tax, and estate planning for more than 30 years. Bob is a Certified Public Accountant, a Personal Financial Specialist, an Accredited Estate Planner, and a Certified Tax Coach. He is a graduate of Arizona State University and Covenant Theological Seminary.

As CEO and President of Eaton Cambridge, Inc., Bob serves as CFO for many of his clients focusing on wealth enhancement (minimizing tax impacting while ensuring desired cash flow), wealth transfer (finding the most tax-efficient ways to pass assets on to succeeding generations), and charitable tax planning (fulfilling charitable goals in the most impactful way possible).

Many also consult Bob for advice on sensitive issues such as coping after the death of a spouse, choosing a nursing home, or facing a lawsuit. Bob is married with seven children and five grandchildren (and counting). He is very involved in ministry at his local church, serving as a spiritual mentor to young men and their families.

CHAPTER 16

The Hunt for the Right Accountant

Starring the Usual Suspects

By Larisa Humphrey, CTC

B y the time you finish this book, you will likely have more knowledge about tax planning than anyone you know. This information is great for more than impressing people at parties: it also helps you learn the basics of establishing a solid financial strategy for your business and planning your retirement. However, no book can turn you into a financial expert. To get the full value from your new knowledge, you will need to partner with someone who is truly experienced in the field of tax planning.

All great detectives work with a partner, and tax detectives are no exception. Before you try to start solving tax mysteries in your own life, it is a good idea to audition a few partners and choose the right one to help you with your investigations.

DIY Accounting Can Cost You Big Money

Just as you didn't become an expert in your field overnight, you can't expect to become a financial guru after learning a few strategies. More importantly, you shouldn't try. After all, you likely already have a business that you are passionate about. It makes more sense to keep your days free to focus on what you are best at while having a professional deal with the financial aspects.

Some people mistakenly believe that they don't need a tax professional because they can file their own taxes. Unfortunately, for them, a piece of accounting software is no substitute for a living, breathing person.

When you file your own taxes, you run the risk of missing crucial pieces of information, simply because you didn't understand what you were doing, or because something didn't seem important at the time. Later, when the notice from the IRS arrives, will you even remember what you did wrong to cause the mistake that is now being pointed out? Even if you file your taxes correctly, you will still likely miss out on opportunities to trim your taxes. Your software isn't likely to prompt you when you are about to miss a money-saving opportunity, but a clever tax coach certainly will. Most people lack either the knowledge or the experience to reduce their tax bills—having someone on hand who knows the tax code inside out allows you to benefit from their expertise.

Opportunity Costs: The Biggest Expense of DIY Accounting

Even if you have filled out all the forms correctly and reported your taxes to the best of your ability, you can still find yourself losing out on valuable opportunities when you try to do it alone in the financial world. Since you are probably not a tax expert, it is unlikely that you know about all of the nuances in the tax code, especially since the laws change frequently.

Taxes are a popular topic of political campaigns, and the laws can change with every election. Investments and tax strategies that were once safe and smart can lose their effectiveness without warning. For example, the Roth IRA is currently one of the most popular types of investments for tax planning since the gains it earns are not taxed. Right now, Roth IRAs are limited to people with incomes below a particular threshold. In the future, these limitations could be changed to become stricter, or Roth IRAs could lose their tax-preferred status.

On the other hand, insurance investments are unlikely to go anywhere. Since life insurance was first developed, the death benefits have been tax-free. The insurance industry is worth billions, and plenty of well-paid lobbyists work hard to make sure that no major changes are made to the way insurance works. A good financial planner would know this and would make plans accordingly. This is just one of the ways that expert knowledge can inform financial decisions; there are many other similar examples that you can find with further investigation into the world of tax law.

This ever-changing financial landscape can represent a challenge to the untrained eye or an opportunity to someone with experience. Knowing how and when to take advantage of a tax opportunity doesn't come naturally to a novice, but missing a valuable chance can be costly.

How Much Is a Lower Tax Bill Worth to You?

There is a great quote from Red Adair that goes, "If you think it is expensive to hire a professional to do the job, wait until you hire an amateur." An amateur may be more affordable up-front, but in the long run, you will end up losing money thanks to mistakes, oversights, or missed opportunities.

This is true whether you are the amateur in question, or you have tried to cut corners by hiring a tax professional who isn't actually experienced in the field. In either case, you will miss out on opportunities, and this can ultimately cost you a lot of money.

The tax strategies highlighted in this book give you the opportunity to save you thousands of dollars every year. Is it worth it to you to pay a few hundred dollars in consultation fees in order to save $5,000 or more in taxes each year? Most smart businesspeople would enthusiastically say yes!

Add to that the time you save by leaving the task to a professional rather than messing with it yourself. When you spend hours trying to sort out your taxes on your own, you are wasting valuable time that could be spent on your business. It is much more efficient to delegate this task to someone who can do it more quickly and effectively, so that you don't lose more time than necessary.

Creative Accounting

Throughout this book, we have investigated many tax mysteries and uncovered some clues toward trimming your tax bill. These are strategies that a creative accountant can employ to solve real problems faced by real business owners. However, not every accountant is going to be willing or able to employ unique methods. Creativity isn't something people usually associate with tax planning. When you think of accountants, most of the time you probably envision people who are very boring and rigid. While this stereotype is true for some, it doesn't describe every accountant. Some financial experts are every bit as creative as artists, and they use that creativity to build smart tax strategies.

Just as all the music in history has been composed of the same 7 notes, and every book in the world was written with the same 26 letters, every tax strategy ultimately makes use of just 4 techniques:

- Shifting: This can mean moving money from a high-tax area like income to a lower-tax category like investing. It could also mean moving money from one investment to another or building a secondary business to reduce your overall tax bracket.

- Timing: The knowledge of when to do things in order to gain the greatest financial impact is vital. This might include knowing when to cash out various investments during retirement or when to sell stocks rather than hold onto them. It can also mean knowing when it is smart to claim a deduction rather than let it roll forward to another year.

- Tax code: Knowing tax laws and identifying loopholes is a crucial part of a tax planner's job. Keeping up with changes in the law, and modifying tax strategies accordingly, is also vital.

- Investments: This category is really made up from elements of the other three techniques. Investing is the most powerful tool at the disposal of anyone looking to save money on taxes because investments are taxed at a preferential rate. You can always benefit from investing rather than earning all of your income through wages.

Creative tax strategies apply these four techniques to a given situation in new, innovative ways in order to get the best possible results.

Choosing the Right Tax Professional

Just as there are no one-size-fits-all tax strategies, no single financial advisor will be perfect for everyone. Some accountants are not comfortable thinking outside the box or applying creative solutions to tax problems. Others may lack experience with your particular industry and overlook valuable opportunities because of it. Some may just be a poor fit for your personality or fail to understand your long-term goals and objectives.

It is worth taking the time to get to know a prospective tax professional to make sure you are choosing the right person to help with your tax planning. After all, your accountant is your partner. He will probably end up learning more about your finances than your spouse, and you will share plenty of personal information with him—from how you plan to spend your retirement, to what you did during business trips. Choosing somebody that you can trust and whose values align with yours is important to achieving the best results.

Tax Planning vs Tax Preparation

When looking for a new accountant or tax professional, it is important to keep your goals in mind. Not everyone who files taxes at the end of the year will be comfortable providing financial advice throughout the year or establishing a tax plan. In fact, the majority of accountants tend to be reactive rather than proactive: they look at your expenses for the year, and point out where you have missed opportunities or made mistakes, but they are not likely to draft a plan for minimizing tax issues in the future.

Tax Preparation

- Is the process of filing taxes at the end of each year.
- Is a reactive process, considering only what you have already done.
- Offers few tax-saving opportunities since money has already been spent.
- Primarily relies on shifting expenses from one category to another or using a different tax form to obtain savings.
- Can be completed by most CPAs and accountants.

Tax Planning

- Is a proactive strategy that looks ahead to devise a plan for future years.
- Advises you on what purchases and investments to make in the upcoming year to save the most on taxes and other expenses.
- Takes advantage of changes in the tax code to keep strategies up to date.
- Requires creative accounting and a financial advisor experienced in proactive financial strategies.

Ideally, you will want a tax professional who is both knowledgeable and experienced in the art of tax planning. You want someone who will help you draft a financial plan for your business, retirement, and investment needs. You will also want someone who will actively work with you throughout the year to be sure that you are on the right track and make adjustments as necessary.

Once you have a tax plan in place, you probably won't need to change it very often. However, current events and changes to the tax code can affect your plan and necessitate an update. You will also need to change your plans from time to time to keep up with your personal situation. For example, retirement planning as a single person is very different than planning as a person with a family to care for and a financial legacy to build. You want a tax planner who is flexible enough to help you through all of these changes and continue modifying your tax strategy to ensure it is the perfect fit for your needs.

Things to Consider When Hiring a New Accountant

Now that you have discovered the importance of a financial planner and investigated some of the ways that tax planning differs from tax preparation, it is time to dig deeper into the mystery of how exactly you go about finding a talented partner for your tax detective journey.

First, you are faced with the decision of what kind of accountant or financial advisor you are looking for. There are plenty of options to choose from. You may find that a Certified Tax Coach is better suited to your needs than a standard CPA. Here are several reasons why:

- Certified Tax Coaches are entrepreneurial in spirit, so they will understand your business goals more intimately than other types of accountants.
- The focus of a CTC is always on proactive tax strategies rather than on reactive approaches.
- The CTC designation signals a specific school of thought when it comes to tax planning, so any Certified Tax Coach will be a good fit for this role; starting with a CTC saves you from wasting time trying to determine how creative a traditional accountant might be with his or her tax strategies.
- Certified Tax Coaches can be found throughout the country, so you don't need to feel wedded to a particular accounting firm. If you move, you can still find a CTC in your new city and feel confident that the new person can help you achieve your goals.

Once you have found a promising potential tax coach, you will want to spend some time getting to know one another. There is nothing wrong with interviewing your new accountant to see whether he or she will be a good fit. Here are a few questions to keep in mind when vetting potential tax advisors:

- Do you have similar philosophies in regards to money? You won't get far if you believe in squeezing every extra cent you can from the IRS if your accountant believes you should pay your fair share without taking advantage of tax loopholes and opportunities.

- Is she comfortable with creative accounting? Some accountants lack creativity and prefer to do things by the book. Others may not feel comfortable thinking outside the box or applying new strategies to your tax plan. Bring up some of the topics described in this book to gauge how comfortable your tax advisor would be with becoming a tax detective.

- Is your financial planner experienced in your industry? Many tax breaks and opportunities are specific to certain types of businesses. Knowing a particular industry intimately means having thorough knowledge of available deductions and loopholes that may not exist for other kinds of businesses.

- Is your accountant knowledgeable about the tax code? Many accountants can get by with knowing just the basics, and their clients might never notice the difference. You don't want someone with just a superficial knowledge of the tax code. You want an expert who knows the law backwards and forwards and is able to apply that knowledge practically to new situations.

- Do you get along well with your prospective tax advisor? You don't necessarily need to be best friends, but you do need to be able to trust each other and feel comfortable sharing your financial information. You should also feel that you can trust the advice your tax planner gives you.

Once you have found a financial advisor who is a good fit for your needs, take some time to sit down, discuss your goals, and start drafting a plan. Together, the two of you should be able to tackle some of the toughest tax mysteries and devise solutions for any problems you run into.

Let's Review Our Clues

- Like every detective, a tax detective needs a good partner to help solve the mysteries of the tax code.

- You can't be expected to be a tax expert on top of everything else you do. It is much more efficient to find a knowledgeable professional and save your time and energy for your passions.

- Tax laws change frequently, especially since tax reform is a popular topic in political elections.

- Staying on top of changes to the tax law is an important part of financial planning.

- Although it can seem cheaper to take a DIY approach to tax planning and preparation, you will actually end up costing yourself more money in the long-term. This is due in part to errors you might make and to missed opportunities for saving money.

- When looking for a financial advisor, you should take the time to make sure the person you are hiring is a good match for your needs and plans.

- Not every accountant will be experienced or comfortable with creative accounting.

- Take some time to get to know an accountant before adding him or her to your team. You should feel comfortable and willing to have a long-term friendly business relationship. You need to be able to trust each other to get the best results.

Once armed with a personalized tax plan, you and your tax coach will become a force to be reckoned with.

ABOUT THE AUTHOR

Larisa Humphrey, CTC

I Paid More Taxes Than a Billionaire!

I am Larisa Humphrey, and I started Abundant Returns Tax Service back in 1991 after seeing on TV that Ross Perot, then presidential candidate and CEO of a multibillion-dollar corporation, paid less than $2,000 in personal income taxes! I just couldn't believe it because…

I made $35,000 that year and paid

More Than $4,000 in federal taxes alone!

I paid more than double the taxes a billionaire paid!

I was flabbergasted, to say the least. "He is a billionaire," I kept saying to myself. "How is it legal for a billionaire to pay less taxes than I do?"

I kept tossing it around in my head; I just couldn't believe it. I worried about how I was going to pay the rent. I struggled to buy a bus pass every week. I had to make arrangements every month to pay my utility bills. My grocery budget was $15/week—and I was paying more income taxes than a billionaire?! It made absolutely no sense to me. And it still makes no sense to me 20 years later! (If I think about it long enough, I still get mad.)

This was an aha moment for me—a life lesson that shattered my very sheltered view of reality. I learned two very valuable lessons: life is not fair, and rich people can avoid income taxes. So I got busy:

- I took several income-tax-preparation courses.
- I read hundreds of books on taxes.
- I prepared thousands of tax returns.

- I worked for the IRS and a local tax office.
- I learned how to use tax law to my advantage.
- I learned how to live tax-free—like billionaires do.

Now I am ready to share that knowledge with you, so you can "Keep More Money In Your Pocket" too. As a medical tax coach, I specialize in preparing tax plans for medical professionals. In my e-book, *Pay Yourself Instead of Uncle Sam*, I explore many tax strategies that will help you reduce your taxes as much as possible. You can find it at www.find-business-tax-deductions.com or www.MedicalTaxCoach.com.

For special offers to readers of this book, and to join my mailing list, go to www.MedicalTaxCoach.com. You can email me at larisa@abundantreturns.com or feel free to give me a call at (770) 451-6330.